THE POWER
OF THE CROSS

THE POWER
OF THE CROSS

PUTTING IT TO WORK IN YOUR LIFE

TONY EVANS

MOODY PUBLISHERS

CHICAGO

Edited by Jim Vincent
Interior design: Ragont Design
Cover design: Thinkpen Design
Cover photo of cross-shaped window copyright © by Alexandra Giese/Shutterstock
(120529090). All rights reserved.

Library of Congress Cataloging-in-Publication Data

Evans, Tony
 The power of the cross / by Anthony T. Evans.
  pages cm
 ISBN 978-0-8024-1118-1
 1. Jesus Christ—Crucifixion. I. Title.
 BT453.E935 2016
 232.96'3—dc23
                                       2015031064

We hope you enjoy this book from Moody Publishers. Our goal is to provide high-
quality, thought-provoking books and products that connect truth to your real needs
and challenges. For more information on other books and products written and
produced from a biblical perspective, go to www.moodypublishers.com or write to:

Moody Publishers
820 N. LaSalle Boulevard
Chicago, IL 60610

1 3 5 7 9 10 8 6 4 2

Printed in the United States of America

To Dr. Charles Ryrie
Thank you for your investment in my life,
education, ministry, and theological perspective.

CONTENTS

INTRODUCTION:

THE CENTERPIECE

AS A BOY GROWING UP in Baltimore, I had a regular Saturday routine. First, I would finish the home chores that my mom had assigned me. Then, when all those duties were done—usually by noon—I would head down to the diamond. The diamond was a large field located just a few minutes from my house where the guys gathered every Saturday to play football..

It was my passion. Even though I played in school during the week as a halfback, and even if there was a Friday night game the evening before, you could still locate me every single Saturday afternoon at the diamond.

On one occasion, we had all gathered at the diamond for our Saturday afternoon games. As we always did, we had chosen sides, and it was time for the game to commence. However, when we started to line up across from each other, we began to look around for the football. We looked for a while, because on this particular Saturday no one had brought a football!

We had taken the time to go to the diamond and had been proactive to choose up teams, yet everything came to an abrupt end simply because the football was not there. We were not able to do what we had gathered to do because the main thing was missing.

Isn't it amazing how something so small can carry so much weight? We couldn't play football without the football.

You see, in the game of football the ball determines everything. First downs are measured by where the ball is placed. Touchdowns are measured by whether the ball crosses the goal line. Fumbles are determined by who grabs the ball. Field goals are measured by whether the ball goes through the goalposts. Men fight over it, rejoice over it, and strive to possess it. The game has spawned a multibillion dollar business enterprise, the National Football League (NFL), that elicits the focus, attention, and adoration of millions of fans each weekend. But if the football is missing, there is no game. Without the football, everything else that goes on in a stadium or on a field is a waste of time.

The Cross: The Main Thing

In Christianity, the cross is the main thing—the centerpiece of the Christian life.

What Jesus gained at the cross is the main thing. Without the crucifixion of Christ on the cross there is no power, no freedom, no forgiveness, no authority, no strength, no victory—nothing at all. The cross is the main thing.

Every year around Easter time, people will typically focus on the cross. We remember that Christ's death paid the penalty for our sins. The cross led to an empty tomb three days later. Resurrection—life everlasting—came because of Christ's sacrificial death. We meditate on how the reality of the cross enables those who believe and trust in Jesus to spend eternity in heaven. However, once Easter passes, we frequently go back to doing our own thing and trying to live our lives without the cross as the central focus.

This makes about as much sense as if the NFL decided to have a football available for the Super Bowl only, and not use any footballs for the other weeks of the season leading up to it. Without a football every week, a football at the Super Bowl isn't going to do you much good, for there would be no Super Bowl.

In the same way it isn't enough to gather together at the right place each Sunday—the church—or with the right people in our lives—fellow believers. And it isn't enough that there is a program or that there are books, seminars, and worship celebrations on Sunday and throughout the week. All of that is good and helpful. But all of that means nothing without the centrality of the main thing—the cross. If we leave out the cross, we are only left with the empty shell called religion.

We are left with an empty set of rules, requirements, and judgments to try and legislate spirituality leaving behind the intimacy, grace, and power to live spiritually victorious lives. As a result, believer after believer finds themselves in perpetual defeat—never measuring up, never fully overcoming their struggles, never rising above their circumstances. They are unable to fulfill their destinies and achieve their own significance because they are operating without the power and deliverance of the

> THE CROSS IS THE GREATEST AFFIRMATION AND DEMONSTRATION OF PURE LOVE.

cross. They are trying to live the Christian life without the main thing— which makes as much sense as trying to play a football game without a football.

Often we will wear the cross around our necks, dangle it from our ears, or hang pictures, banners, and replicas of it within our homes and churches. Yet in doing so we run the risk of detaching the cross from its true meaning and power. We run the risk of belittling its authentic strength. We may turn it into a good luck charm or decoration. Essentially, we can make the cross nothing more than a replica to induce guilt rather than announce what it is: the single greatest affirmation and demonstration of pure love.

The problem in our personal lives, homes, churches, and communities today is not a lack of knowledge or skills. It is not even entirely a problem of a lack of motivation. In our contemporary Christian culture the problem is that we have forgotten the purpose, preeminence, and the power of the cross. We view it as an icon that has little relevance to us today other than at Communion or Easter.

Rather than viewing the cross as an icon reflecting something that happened thousands of years ago, we ought to view it as a historical event that will take us to heaven—a current event containing everything we need to bring heaven to bear on earth.

Paul: Remember Christ and the Cross

In writing to his audience at Galatia, the apostle Paul urged them over and over, in one form or another, to remember Christ and the cross. As Paul concluded his letter to those in the Galatian church, he did what we will often do today through the use of italics, underlining, or bolding; he emphasized his point by writing largely. It says that Paul wrote in "large letters . . . with [his] own hand" (Galatians 6:11). In essence Paul said, "I don't want you to miss this part. I know that everything I've said up until now has been important, but this part is the most important part."

He reminded them of the cross, his only hope of achievement: "But may it never be that I would boast, except in the cross of our Lord Jesus Christ, through which the world has been crucified to me, and I to the world."

Paul had been saved for some time, yet he was still saying, "I'm only going to brag on the cross." He did not let the historical reality of the cross lose its contemporary relevance. Paul's only point of reference for his life was the cross. The cross was central to his very existence. It was the power to overcome his weaknesses. It was his identity and his hope.

Religion or Relationship?

The reason Paul spent so much effort focusing on the cross in his letter to the Galatians was because they had become confused about what true spirituality and power meant. They were no longer looking to the power provided them through Christ's death on the cross and the sending of the Holy Spirit; rather, they were looking to themselves, to what they could do instead of what Christ already did. Paul was keenly aware of how this mindset had crept into the hearts of the Galatians. Thus he wrote a few chapters later, "Those who desire to make a good showing in the flesh try to compel you to be circumcised, simply so that they will not be persecuted for the cross of Christ" (Galatians 6:12).

Paul was saying that what was keeping the Christians in Galatia from experiencing the fullness of Jesus Christ, as well as living out the abundance of the Christian experience, was religion. Religion had gotten in the way of the cross.

In that day, circumcision was the external symbol of religious commitment and involvement. In fact, a specific group of people would follow Paul around, and whenever he would start a church they would try to change the belief structure of the church. Known as the "Judaizers" (from the Greek verb *ioudaïzō*, which means "live according to Jewish customs"), they were still attached to the religious rules of the Old Testament. Those Judaizers would try to convince the new Christians to conform to external religious observances, of which circumcision was the chief observance. They were trying to subvert the message of the cross.

They had religion. They just didn't have a relationship with Jesus Christ.

Yet whenever religious activity, however sincere, trumps relationship, the power of Jesus Christ is no longer experienced in the believer's life.

One of the greatest dangers in our churches today is for religion to replace an intimate relationship with the Savior. *Religion* is the external adherence to exercises, codes, or standards in the name of God yet apart from God. For example, if you go to church because it is the religious, or spiritual, thing to do rather than because you are motivated to spend time worshiping God, learning about Him, and experiencing Him, then that is religion. Religion is anything you do for God that does not stem out of a heart connected to God.

I remember one particular research paper I prepared in seminary. When I turned it in I was very proud of the work I had put into it. I had done my due diligence. I had controlled the material and analyzed all of the possible idiosyncratic elements of the arguments. I felt great about my paper.

> LEGALISM MEASURES YOUR SPIRITUALITY BY YOUR ACTIVITY. YOU MUST ALWAYS DO MORE, BE BETTER, AND STRIVE HARDER.

However, when I got my paper back from my professor, there was a big, fat, red zero at the top, along with a smaller note at the bottom. In a hurried hand, my professor had scrawled, "Tony, great work. Great preparation. Wrong assignment."

It wasn't that I hadn't done great work; it was that I had done my great work on the wrong assignment. I had researched the wrong topic. As a result, I didn't get credit for what I had done. Christianity is no different. It's not that there aren't a lot of people doing a lot of excellent things. It's not that a lot of these same people attend church, help the hurting, or say all the correct spiritual platitudes. It's just in their good activities they've missed the cross. They've missed Jesus Christ. And then they wonder why they aren't experiencing any victory, power, hope, and authority.

The reason is that external observances—the rules of religion—can actually get in the way of a relationship. Often these religious rules are termed *legalism*. What legalism does is measures your spirituality by your activity. Within legalism, you must always do more, be better, go further, pray longer, and strive harder. The list goes on and on. One of the problems with legalism is that you never know when you get to the end of the list because there is always something else to add to it.

Paul wrote stern words to those contemplating following the Judaizers' path of religion in Galatians 5: "It was for freedom that Christ set us free; therefore keep standing firm and do not be subject again to a yoke of slavery. . . . if you receive circumcision, Christ will be of no benefit to you. . . . You have been severed from Christ, you who are seeking to be justified by law; you have fallen from grace" (vv. 1–2, 4).

Paul uses the terms "severed from Christ" and "fallen from grace" to indicate that Jesus Christ is no longer of any benefit to you on earth. His strength, intimacy, power, and all that He has to offer has been removed from you if you are counting on yourself to be religious. The profundity of this truth is serious: Paul is saying that religious activity can actually keep Christians from experiencing the Lord. Church activity can actually keep us from Christ. Self-righteousness can keep us from true righteousness.

For example, a married woman checking off a list of things to do in her home because she is under pressure, seeking approval, or is intimidated by her husband reflects a far different relationship than a married woman who does the same list because she is motivated by love. The activity may be the same; in fact, it could be identical. But the motivation changes both the enjoyment and rewards of the activity.

God doesn't want us serving Him only because we are supposed to. He also wants us serving Him because we want to, pure and simple. He wants our heart. He wants our morality, prayer life, dedication for Him, and all else to be predicated on your relationship with Him rather than on religious duty. Instead of being defined by what you do, He wants you to be defined by who you belong to—Jesus Christ.

Two Crucifixions

The apostle Paul describes two crucifixions that must occur on the cross in order to live a victorious Christian life—Jesus' and your own. He writes of himself, "But may it never be that I would boast, except in the cross of our Lord Jesus Christ, through which the world has been crucified to me, and I to the world" (Galatians 6:14).

In other words, on the cross, Paul was crucified to all things that belong to this world. Being "crucified" with Christ, Paul had (1) a resulting disconnect from this world's order and (2) a subsequent attachment and alignment with Christ. These are the two crucifixions.

The word "world" in the Greek is *kosmos*. It simply refers to an organized world system or arrangement designed to promote a specific emphasis or philosophy. For example, we will often talk about the "world of sports," the "world of finance," or the "world of politics." These phrases are not referencing a location or a place. They are referencing an organized system inclusive of certain definitions, regulations, and philosophical worldviews.

When Paul states that he has been crucified with Christ, he is saying that he is no longer alive to this world's system that wants to leave God out, sometimes known as "worldliness." The apostle writes that he has been crucified to the strategies and rules that are set up to try to make humanity acceptable to God independently of God.

This world really does not mind religion. The world not only tolerates religion, it frequently will even embrace it. Religions dominate much of humanity's systems all across the globe. What the world will not tolerate, however, is the cross of Jesus Christ. As soon as you introduce Jesus into the equation, you have become too specific. Staying with God is okay because that is generic and vague.

The Cross as Our Central Focus

Remember, the cross is not about religion. It is an expression of an undying love and the payment for all of mankind's sin—past, present, and future. Including yours.

If something happens to the hub of a wheel, the spokes become disconnected. Similarly, if you fail to make the cross the central focus of your life—your identity in Christ—you run the risk of experiencing extreme disconnection in the various areas of what you do. Don't allow the world system that leaves God out to define you. Be cautious not to be duped into believing that you can make it dipping in and out of both.

Have you ever gone swimming in a lake or in the ocean that was very deep? If you chose to swim one hundred feet below the surface, you wouldn't survive, simply because your body was not made for that environment. Without the proper equipment, you might last two minutes. Friend, the cross is your equipment in this world. It is your oxygen tank. It is your identity. It is your point of reference. It is your life. It is all of that.

Why do so many believers struggle to live victorious lives? Because they accept the cross but then leave the cross behind. Jesus said, "Whoever wants to be my disciple must deny themselves and take up their cross and follow me" (Matthew 16:24 NIV). He didn't say that you are to pick up your cross and then set it back down. He said you are to carry it with you.

This is an ongoing identification,w as Paul pointed out in his letter to the Corinthians where he said, "I affirm, brethren, by the boasting in you which I have in Christ Jesus our Lord, *I die daily*" (1 Corinthians 15:31, italics added). The cross represents the moment-by-moment connection to and identification with Jesus Christ and the purpose of His life, death, burial, and resurrection. It is acknowledgment of complete and total dependency on Christ and His sufficiency, along with a recognition of personal sin.

Jesus wants to be more important to you than your own comforts. He told the curious crowd, "Whoever does not carry his own cross and come after Me cannot be My disciple" (Luke 14:27). You must carry *your* cross, not Jesus' cross. He took care of His own. You need to carry your cross.

Carrying Your Cross

We have some messed-up ideas about what it means to carry our crosses. Some say when they have a physical problem, bad in-laws, or noisy neighbors, "Well, I have to bear my cross." None of those situations is a cross.

In Roman times, a convict made to carry his cross to the place of execution was saying to the public he was guilty of a great crime. To carry your cross today means to bear the reproach of Jesus Christ. It is to be so identified with Him that when they accuse you of being a Christian, you are found guilty. When someone accuses you of being His disciple, you say, "You got me." To carry your own cross is to admit publicly that you are committed to Christ, guilty of placing Him first.

Carrying your cross is when a girl tells her boyfriend, "I can't sleep with you because I am a Christian." It's when a businessman says, "I can't do that unethical thing, because I am Christ's disciple. I am living by a different agenda." Carrying your cross is dying to yourself and what you want and putting Jesus first. It's not comfortable to carry a cross.

Religion and religious titles mean nothing. What matters is your identification with Jesus Christ and the newness of the life within you. The apostle Paul told the Corinthian believers, "Therefore if anyone is in Christ, he is a new creature; the old things passed away; behold, new things have come" (2 Corinthians 5:17).

Victory in your daily life, decisions, emotions, finances, and in all things hinges on your attachment to Jesus Christ and what He did at the cross. It rests on His work, not on your own. It is tied to the new creation within you, not to the flesh.

Paul concludes his letter to the believers in Galatia with this final thought reflecting on the fruit of a life connected to the cross: "Those who will walk by this rule, peace and mercy be upon them" (Galatians 6:16). Why do so many people lack peace in their lives today? Because they are failing to align themselves under the perfect power of the cross.

Paul says that if you walk according to the rule of the cross, that is, if you align your frame of thinking and operating with the centrality of the cross, you will experience the benefits of God, which include peace and mercy. However, when you are merely satisfied with religion or religious activity—or even when you have placed your trust in your religious activity to earn favor with God—you have been severed from Christ, and fallen from grace.

Fallen from grace is a fairly drastic occurrence. Grace is the provision of all that you need in order to live a life of abundance and peace. To best understand what it means to be "severed from Christ" or to be "fallen from grace," I need to compare it to electricity. Electricity is the flow of power that makes everything work in your home. Virtually everything in your house operates because of electricity. Your appliances, lights, heat, air-conditioning, computers, and television all work because they are receiving electricity. If you are severed from electricity, the flow of the power stops even though you have those appliances and lights.

To be severed from Christ or to fall from grace means that the flow of what God wants to do in you and through you has stopped. You have essentially been unplugged, or disconnected, from the power of Jesus even though you still have all of the paraphernalia of religion. Therefore, you lose hope, you lack peace, your courage wanes, and your faith shakes.

Yet those who function by the rule of the cross will experience a peace that passes understanding. The Spirit of God will permeate all that you do so much so that you begin to think differently, live differently, and love differently. This is because the flow of the Spirit, the electricity that comes to each of us by way of the accomplishment of the cross, will empower you. God will be at work in you.

Never let religion get in the way of your relationship with Jesus Christ. Rather, take the cross off from around your neck and carry it instead. You have been crucified with Christ in order to live like the new creation you truly are.

Looking Ahead

To help you on this path of new discovery in incorporating the *person*, *purpose*, and *power* of the cross in your life, in parts 1–3 we will dig deep into each of these topics. We will begin by looking at the person of Jesus Christ—what makes Him unique, how He was announced ahead of time through both prophecy and typology, as well as how His humiliation, death, and resurrection set Him apart as Lord over all.

Then we'll move into a look at the purpose of the cross—what was accomplished on it for us, how it is designed to be positioned as the centerpiece of our lives, and the authority it not only is to have but offers to us as well.

Finally, we will study the power of the cross in your everyday life, including the stability it provides, the deliverance it offers, and the power of its ongoing remembrance.

I congratulate you for choosing this path of study in order to acquaint yourself with everything God has done and thus offers through His Son and His death on the cross.

PART 1

THE PERSON
OF THE CROSS

1

THE UNIQUENESS

JESUS CHRIST IS the one-of-a-kind person in all of history. Jesus of Nazareth, the unique One, has undoubtedly been the subject of more books, more songs, and more devotion than anyone who has ever lived. His appearance on earth was so monumental that history divided around His life, before Christ (BC) and in the year of our Lord (*anno Domini*, or AD). Time has meaning to us as it is defined by the presence of Jesus Christ in history.

On one occasion Jesus' disciples voiced the question that people have continued to ask about Him for almost two thousand years. Having witnessed His miraculous calming of the sea, the Twelve looked at each other and asked, "What kind of a man is this?" (Matthew 8:27). In other words, who is this Jesus? The Gospels and the rest of the New Testament were written to answer that question and explain its implications for our lives.

In part 1 we will explore this greatest of all subjects, considering the uniqueness and authority of Jesus and then looking more deeply at His death and resurrection.

His Unique Identity

Jesus is unique because He is the only person who existed before He was born (see John 1:1, 14) and who is today what He has always been (Hebrews 13:8). That makes him *Deity*. But He is more than Deity. He is the only person whose earthly conception had no relationship to His origin. By virtue of His birth as a man, Jesus Christ is now *both Son of God and Son of Man*. He is Deity and He is humanity. He is the God-man—Deity incarnated, given flesh.

His nature is "very God of very God," to use a phrase theologians coined to try to declare Christ's divine nature. A lot of people respect Jesus Christ as a great person, an inspiring teacher, and a great leader, but reject His deity.

This is heresy. You cannot hold Jesus in high regard while denying He is the eternal God, a point Jesus Himself made clear to the religious rulers, the crowds, and His closest disciples (for example, John 8:23–24, 28–29; 10:30–37).

Jesus Christ clearly and directly claimed to be God when He said, "I and the Father are one" (John 10:30). This statement is significant because the word "one" is neuter in form, meaning that He and the Father are one, perfect in nature and unified in essence. This was a personal claim of total equality with the Father. Those who heard this statement clearly understood it to be a claim to deity, for they immediately tried to stone Him for blasphemy because He made Himself equal to God (v. 33).

Four Proofs of His Deity

We could use a number of lines of argument to demonstrate Jesus' deity but I want to consider four of them, beginning with His *preexistence*. We have already said that Christ existed before His birth. The prophet Micah stated Christ's preexistence this way: "As for you, Bethlehem Ephrathah, too little to be among the clans of Judah, from you One will go forth for Me to be ruler in Israel. His goings forth are from long ago, from the days of eternity" (5:2).

This is a significant verse for several reasons, beginning with Micah's accuracy in prophesying Jesus' birthplace. I have visited Bethlehem, and even today it's a small town. Yet it was even smaller and more insignificant in Jesus' day, so for Micah to predict Bethlehem as Messiah's birthplace was more surprising, like telling readers where to find a needle in a haystack. But notice what the prophet said about this One who would be born in Bethlehem. He had no beginning; His existence reaches back into eternity past.

Likewise, the prophet Isaiah gave Jesus Christ the title "Eternal Father" (9:6), or "Father of eternity," in his prophecy of Jesus' first and second comings. Since Jesus is the Father of eternity, He is also the Father or initiator of time. But the only way Jesus could be the initiator of time is if He existed before time. This verse speaks of His preexistence and tells us that Christ is of a different nature than anyone who has ever lived.

The prophets were not the only ones who taught Jesus' preexistence. Jesus declared it Himself in an exchange that stunned and infuriated His Jewish detractors. They had accused Jesus of having a demon (John 8:52) because He claimed that anyone who believed in Him would not see death. They reviled Him and asked this question: "Whom do You make Yourself out to be?" (v. 53). That's a great question, but they didn't like Jesus' answer, especially when He said, "Your father Abraham rejoiced to see My day" (v. 56).

The Jewish leaders replied, "You are not yet fifty years old, and have You seen Abraham?" (v. 57). They were getting upset because Jesus was making claims no man had ever made before. Then Jesus made this crucial statement: "Truly, truly, I say to you, before Abraham was born, I am" (v. 58).

Don't miss the importance of the verb tenses Jesus used here. He was making a crucial claim. He did not say, "Before Abraham was born, I was" but "I am." This is significant because "I AM" is the name God gave Himself when He sent Moses to redeem Israel from Egypt.

> BY TAKING TO HIMSELF THE MOST PERSONAL AND HALLOWED NAME OF GOD, JESUS WAS MAKING HIMSELF EQUAL WITH GOD.

"God said to Moses . . . 'Thus you shall say to the sons of Israel, "I AM has sent me to you"'" (Exodus 3:14). This is the term we transliterate as "Yahweh," the self-existing God. This name describes God's personal, self-sufficient, and eternal nature. The eternal God has no past, so He cannot say "I was." He has no future, so He cannot say "I will be." God exists in an eternal now.

Time is only meaningful to us because we are not independently self-sufficient and eternal. When Jesus told the Jews that He predated Abraham, He was claiming not only preexistence but Deity.

The second proof of Jesus' deity was He made Himself equal to God. By taking to Himself the most personal and hallowed name of God, "I am" in John 8:58, Jesus claimed equality with God. His hearers understood this perfectly, for on this occasion as well they picked up stones intending to stone Jesus for blasphemy (v. 59).

Jesus' claim is even stronger in John 5:17–18. "'My Father is working until now, and I Myself am working.' For this reason therefore the Jews were seeking all the more to kill Him, because He not only was breaking the Sabbath, but also was calling God His own Father, making Himself equal with God." Those around Him understood Jesus to mean that He was placing Himself on equal standing with God because He was claiming to be of the same essence as God.

The Bible elsewhere equates Jesus with God. Genesis 1:1 says that God created the world. But Colossians 1:16 says that by Jesus Christ, "all things were created." Either we have two Creators, or the God of Genesis 1 is the God of Colossians 1.

The apostle John made the identical claim for Jesus when he began his gospel by declaring, "In the beginning was the Word, and the Word was with God, and the Word was God" (John 1:1). So the Word is distinct from God, yet the Word is equal with God.

John doesn't leave us in doubt about the identity of the Word. "And the Word became flesh, and dwelt among us, and we saw His glory, glory as of the only begotten from the Father, full of grace and truth" (John 1:14). Then he added, "No one has seen God at any time; the only begotten God who is in the bosom of the Father, He has explained Him" (v. 18).

When you put these three verses together, you get quite a picture of Jesus Christ. He is distinct from God, yet equal with God. He took on human flesh for the purpose of making the invisible God visible to human beings. The writer of Hebrews said that Jesus "is the radiance of [God's] glory and the exact representation of His nature, and upholds all things by the word of His power" (Hebrews 1:3).

> IN HEBREWS 1:8 GOD THE FATHER CALLS HIS SON "GOD." NOTHING COULD BE CLEARER THAN THAT.

So don't let anyone tell you that Jesus is just a great man or merely a son of God. He is God, the Son. There is even stronger language in Hebrews 1:8, because here God Himself is the speaker. "Of the Son He says, 'Thy throne, O God, is forever and ever.'" God the Father is calling His Son "God." Nothing could be clearer or more direct than that. No wonder Paul wrote that in Jesus, "All the fullness of Deity dwells in bodily form" (Colossians 2:9).

This cannot be said about anyone else. Jesus claimed equality with God, and the writers of Scripture consistently support that claim.

A third proof for Jesus' deity is that Jesus readily accepted the worship of His disciples and others. For a mere human being to do that would be blasphemy. But Jesus' disciples came to recognize Him as God, and after Jesus' resurrection and ascension, they had no hesitation in making that known.

One example of this worship is that great scene in John 20 when Jesus appeared to the disciples after His resurrection. Thomas had been absent during an earlier visit, and he said he would not believe unless he saw with his own eyes (v. 25). So Jesus came to the disciples and invited Thomas to touch His hands and side and to believe (v. 27). Thomas responded, "My Lord and my God!" (v. 28).

Not only did Jesus accept Thomas's declaration of worship, but He said that all those who believe in Him are "blessed" (v. 29). Notice that when Thomas said, "My Lord and my God," Jesus said in effect, "Yes, I am He." He accepted the worship that is due to Deity alone. We can see worship being offered to Jesus throughout the Gospels. Earlier in Jesus' ministry, the disciples worshiped Him after He calmed a storm (Matthew 14:33). Even demons acknowledged His deity, although Jesus silenced them (Mark 1:23–25). But Jesus Himself offered the strongest proof of His deity. He answered Satan's temptation with the statement, "Go, Satan! For it is written, 'You shall worship the Lord your God, and serve Him only'" (Matthew 4:10).

Jesus said worship belongs to God alone, yet He received that worship. Only God could say what Jesus said.

A fourth proof of Jesus' deity is His membership in the Trinity. Titus 2:13 tells us that Jesus Christ is "our great God and Savior." The Bible teaches that Jesus Christ is the Son of God, and yet He is fully God. It also teaches that God the Father is God. The question the early church grappled with was how Jesus could be God yet also be distinct from the Father as the Son.

A child at our church once asked me, "Pastor, if Jesus is God, then who was He talking to on the cross when He said, 'My God, My God, why have you forsaken Me?' Was He talking to Himself?"

That's a very perceptive question. Jesus was not talking to Himself on the cross but to the Father. We can say this with confidence because the Bible teaches that the Godhead is composed of three distinct, yet coequal persons who share the same divine substance: Father, Son, and Holy Spirit. The term "trinity" is used for this foundational truth.

So when we talk about God, we could be talking about either the Godhead corporately or about any one of the three persons who make up the Godhead. God's Word teaches Jesus' deity because it presents Him as a member of the Godhead, the divine Trinity. Jesus identified Himself as distinct from the Father when Jesus called Himself "the Son of God" (John 10:36). Yet, just a few minutes before He said that, He also said, "I and the Father are one" (v. 30).

The unity of the Trinity and yet the distinction of its three members is evident in Jesus' commission to His disciples. He told us to baptize people "in the name of the Father and the Son and the Holy Spirit" (Matthew 28:19). Normally we would expect to read the plural form "names" here, because Jesus mentioned three names. But He used the singular "name." So we must conclude either that Jesus was mistaken, or that He used the singular on purpose because the three members of the Godhead make up one entity.

There's no question which of these conclusions is correct. The name of God is singular because the triune God is one God. This is the consistent teaching of Scripture. Paul closed one of his letters with this benediction: "The grace of the Lord Jesus Christ, and the love of God, and the fellowship of the Holy Spirit, be with you all" (2 Corinthians 13:14). Paul integrated the three persons of the Godhead because they are one.

The Trinity is not an easy concept to grasp because there is nothing like it in the universe. Without the Bible we would have no knowledge of this kind of existence. It is outside our realm of understanding to think of one God existing in three equal persons who are distinct personalities while sharing the same essence. There have been a number of illustrations suggested for the Trinity, but they all fall short of the mark because the Trinity is unique.

For example, someone has suggested the illustration of water, ice, and steam. All are made up of the same essence, yet they are distinct forms of that essence. The problem with this is that if we apply it to the Godhead, it makes it appear that God appears sometimes as Father, sometimes as Son, and sometimes as Spirit. But that is a heresy because the fullness of the Godhead is always present in each member of the Trinity.

Another common illustration of the Trinity is the egg. An egg has three parts—the shell, the yolk, and the white (albumen). The problem with this illustration is that none of these three parts by itself can be defined as an egg. They are just part of the egg. But the fullness of Deity resides in each individual member of the Godhead. Jesus Christ isn't part God; He is fully God. The same can be said of the Father and the Holy Spirit.

The best illustration I have come up with for the Trinity is a pretzel. A typical pretzel has three circles or holes formed by the dough. These holes are distinct from one another, and each hole is complete within itself. Yet the three holes are interconnected because they belong to the same piece of dough. They have the same character. There is only one pretzel, not three. This is not a perfect illustration, but I think it gets closer to the point. The biblical doctrine of the Trinity establishes the full deity of Jesus Christ. He is God.

The Human God

Yet Jesus is also man. He partakes of the nature of Deity because He is the Son of God. He also partakes of the nature of humanity because He is the "Son of Man." In fact, this was Jesus' favorite title for Himself.

Jesus left heaven to take on human flesh, which is what we mean by the term "incarnation." Jesus became flesh and blood, an event that was prophesied in Scripture hundreds of years before Jesus was born. Two prophecies from the book of Isaiah and their fulfillment in the New Testament give us a picture of Jesus' human nature. He was fully human yet unique in several important ways.

The most important distinctive of Jesus' human nature is that He was born of a virgin. In Isaiah 7:14 the prophet wrote, "The Lord Himself will give you a sign: Behold, a virgin will be with child and bear a son, and she will call His name Immanuel." Two chapters later comes a second prophecy: "A child will be born to us, a son will be given to us" (9:6).

Notice how careful the Holy Spirit is with the language here. The Son is "given," not born. Why? Because as the Son of God, Jesus already existed. But the child is "born," a reference to Jesus' birth in Bethlehem. God the Father gave the Son to us through a supernaturally wrought conception in human flesh through the process of a human birth. Paul brought these prophecies from Isaiah together when he wrote, "When the fullness of the time came, God sent forth His Son, born of a woman, born under the Law" (Galatians 4:4).

God "sent forth" the Son because the Son is given (Isaiah 9:6). Jesus was "born of a woman" because a child was to be born. This is the incarnation of Jesus Christ. The story of Jesus' birth confirms His distinctiveness as God in the flesh. Matthew says that the events of Jesus' birth happened "to fulfill what was spoken by the Lord through the prophet [that is, Isaiah]" (Matthew 1:22). Matthew preceded this statement with the specific reason for Christ's birth, "You shall call His name Jesus, for He will save His people from their sins" (Matthew 1:21).

Essentially, Jesus was a baby who was born to die. Mary knew this. Joseph knew this. Even the wise men who came to worship the child in the cradle who had created them knew this. That's why the gifts they gave Him were gold, frankincense, and myrrh. The myrrh, in particular, is an expensive resin used as a perfume yet also used in burying the dead (John 19:39). The wise men gave Jesus this burial fragrance for the same reason Mary wrapped her newborn in swaddling clothes. Swaddling clothes kept a newborn's arms straight during his or her early days. The strips of cloth were not unlike the bandages used to wrap the dead. The meaning of both the swaddling clothes and the myrrh was not lost on Matthew, who had let us know that this baby had come to take away the sins of the world.

Significantly, the gospel writer earlier gave another testimony to the distinctiveness of Jesus' human nature. Matthew concluded the Lord's genealogy, writing, "Jacob was the father of Joseph the husband of Mary, by whom Jesus was born, who is called the Messiah" (Matthew 1:16). The phrase "by whom" is critical here, because it is a feminine singular relative pronoun. That is very important because the Bible is saying that Jesus was conceived through Mary, but not by Joseph.

This, in other words, is a careful witness to His virgin birth. Joseph is important in Jesus' genealogy, because Matthew is showing that Joseph was descended from David. Since Joseph was Jesus' legal—though not biological—father, Jesus had a rightful claim to the throne of David. Jesus was conceived by the Holy Spirit (Luke 1:35), and not by Joseph, in order that His human nature might be sinless. This is why He would be called "the Son of God" at His birth.

Jesus' humanity had both a heavenly origin through the power of the Holy Spirit and an earthly origin through Mary. Because Jesus' nature is different from ours in terms of being sinless and born of a virgin, some people in church history denied His humanity was real. They believed He just appeared to be human. But that is another heresy that denies the reality of His life and His death for sin.

> JESUS WAS FULLY HUMAN. HE COULD BE TIRED AND THIRSTY, HAD HUMAN EMOTIONS, AND WEPT AT LAZARUS'S GRAVE.

Make no mistake; Jesus was fully human. The Gospels demonstrate this again and again. He was the God who made everything, the God who never becomes weary or needs to sleep. Yet in His humanity He could be tired and thirsty (John 4:6–7). We know Jesus had human emotions because He wept at Lazarus's grave (John 11:35) and felt compassion for people (Matthew 9:36). He also loved us with an everlasting love. And He had a human soul and spirit (Matthew 26:38; Luke 23:46), which all human beings have.

Some people have a problem with Jesus' human nature because they assume if He was human, He had to be sinful. Not when the Holy Spirit oversees the birth process. We have already noted that Jesus was conceived by the Holy Spirit, bypassing the sinful human nature of Joseph as the father. The same objection is raised about the Bible. If human beings wrote the Bible, the argument goes, it must have errors in it. That might be true except for one thing: The Holy Spirit oversaw the writing of Scripture to preserve it from error (2 Peter 1:21).

What the Spirit did with the written Word of God, He did with the incarnate Word of God, Jesus Christ. The Spirit superintended the conception of both the written and the incarnate Word so that there was no human contamination in either. Paul wrote that Jesus "knew no sin," a perfect sacrifice to become "sin on our behalf" so we might partake of God's righteousness (2 Corinthians 5:21).

If Jesus were just a sinful human being, His death would have done nothing to save us. According to Hebrews 4:15, Jesus' present ministry in heaven as our Great High Priest depends upon His sinlessness. He could not help us in our weakness if He were as sinful and weak as we are.

Jesus' Deity and Humanity

The two natures of Jesus Christ form what theologians call *the hypostatic union*. This is a big term that simply means undiminished Deity and perfect humanity united yet unmixed forever in one person. In other words, Jesus was no less God when He became a perfect man. He was fully human, but without sin. It's important that we understand Jesus is one person, not two. He is the God-man, not sometimes God and sometimes man. He is one person with two natures. Jesus has a perfect human and divine nature, which makes Him unique. Nobody else is God become a man—God in the flesh.

One Scripture passage puts all of this together: Philippians 2:5–11. We will deal with this phenomenal passage in greater detail later, but we conclude this chapter with the highlights of this union to show that this passage teaches us how we should live in response to what Jesus did in taking on human nature. Significantly in verses 3–4 the apostle Paul prefaced this passage by calling believers to be humble rather than prideful, to be concerned about the interests of others rather than just their own interests—which is the way Jesus lived when He came to earth.

Then he wrote, "Have this attitude in yourselves which was also in Christ Jesus, who, although He existed in the form of God, did not regard equality with God a thing to be grasped" (vv. 5–6). This is a tremendous statement of Jesus' deity. He existed as God prior to His birth in Bethlehem. He was equal with the Father in divine essence. Here is a succinct statement of what the Bible says about Jesus' deity.

Then we come to Jesus' humanity. He "emptied Himself, taking the form of a bond-servant, and being made in the likeness of men" (v. 7). Does this mean that Jesus emptied Himself of His deity? Not at all. It was impossible that Jesus Christ could cease being God. This verse is not talking about what Jesus emptied Himself of but what He emptied Himself into. It's like pouring something from one pitcher into another. Jesus took all of His deity and poured it into another vessel, the "form of a bond-servant."

He didn't stop being who He is, but He changed the form of who He is. When He came to earth, Jesus moved from His preexistent, glorified form and poured the fullness of His deity into a human form. Simply becoming a human being was enough of a step down for the Son of God. But Jesus became a "bond-servant," a slave, the lowest possible position on the social ladder in that day.

> **JESUS CAME AS A LOWLY SERVANT, WHICH MEANS THERE IS NO ONE WITH WHOM JESUS CANNOT IDENTIFY.**

We could say that He who is very God of very God became "very slave of very slave." That's why most of the people in Jesus' day missed His birth. They were looking for a king, not a servant. They expected a king to be born in a palace to rich parents, not in a stable to the poorest of the poor.

Jesus came as a lowly servant, which is good news for us because that means there is no one with whom Jesus cannot identify. If you are not very high on the social ladder, Jesus understands because He has been there. And no matter how high you may be, Jesus has been higher because He is the Son of God.

When Jesus took on flesh, He was "made in the likeness of men" (Philippians 2:7). Even though Jesus was much more than just a man, those who saw Him regarded Him as just a man. Jesus didn't go around with a halo around His head. He looked like a man.

Luke 2:52 says Jesus grew in the same ways as other people: physically, spiritually, emotionally, and socially. Isaiah said Jesus had "no stately form or majesty" in His human appearance that would make people stop and look twice (53:2). Jesus was not only born in humble circumstances, but "He humbled Himself by becoming obedient to the point of death, even death on a cross" (Philippians 2:8).

In His sacrifice for our sins, Jesus humbly accepted the most painful, humiliating form of death the Romans could inflict. In Jesus' crucifixion we get an idea of what is meant when the Bible says He emptied Himself. Jesus chose to lay aside the independent use of His divine attributes, submitting Himself completely to His Father's will. How do we know this? Because when Peter attacked the high priest's servant, Jesus told Peter He could call more than twelve legions of angels to His defense if He desired (Matthew 26:53). But Jesus did not do that, knowing an effective sacrifice for sin meant that He must suffer and die. He could not simply call on His divine power to wipe out Satan but had to submit Himself to death.

Of course Philippians 2 does not end with verse 8. Because Jesus was obedient to death, "God highly exalted Him, and bestowed on Him the name which is above every name, so that at the name of Jesus every knee will bow . . . and that every tongue will confess that Jesus Christ is

Lord, to the glory of God the Father" (vv. 9–11).

The honor Jesus Christ commands is intrinsic honor, for Jesus is King of the universe, the unique God-man to whom every knee will someday bow. In truly understanding and knowing who He is we are best able to comprehend all that has been accomplished for us on the cross. The cross was not something that just happened at a point in history. Rather, by looking at the prophetic Word we can see how the event of the cross had been established long before Christ was ever even born. Both prophecy and typology pointed forward to it in the Old Testament, which is the subject of our next chapter.

2

THE FORETELLING

SINCE JESUS CHRIST is the focal point of everything God is doing in the world, we would expect Jesus to occupy a unique place in Bible prophecy. And He does. Prophecy foretells the coming of Christ the first time to be the Savior from sin and the second time to rule as King. Prophecy is found in both the Old and New Testaments.

The central truths of prophecies concerning Jesus Christ are that He is both the prophesied Messiah of the Old Testament and the prophesied King who will rule not only over Israel but the entire world. John the Baptist asked the key prophetic question when he sent some disciples from his prison cell to ask Jesus, "Are You the Expected One, or do we look for someone else?" (Luke 7:19).

John was asking Jesus if He was the prophesied Messiah. If not, John and his disciples needed to be doing something else and looking elsewhere for God's redemption. Prophecy is critical to our understanding of who Jesus Christ is.

My purpose here is not to deal with every prophecy in Scripture related to Jesus. That would take a book in itself. My purpose is to show you that Jesus is the focus of Bible prophecy and this makes His death on the cross, and what it achieved, a matter of great importance.

Christ Himself teaches about His central place in prophecy during

a walk with two of His disciples to the village of Emmaus the very evening of resurrection day (Luke 24:13–27). Later that night Jesus would
appear to His eleven closest disciples and other disciples and teach further truth concerning Himself.

The whole town was in pandemonium over Jesus, who was called
"King of the Jews" and who claimed to be the Son of God, but who had
been crucified a few days earlier. Now it was reported that He was alive
again. His grave was empty. No wonder there was no place a person
could go in Jerusalem where people were not discussing Jesus. So it
was natural that these two disciples would be reviewing events of this
incredible weekend on their way home.

As they walked, "Jesus Himself approached and began traveling
with them. But their eyes were prevented from recognizing Him" (Luke
24:15–16). Jesus asked them, "What are these words that you are exchanging with one another?" (v. 17).

Getting the Big Picture

Cleopas (v. 18) and the other disciple must have been having quite a
discussion, because the word "exchanging" means a heated debate. They
couldn't believe this apparent stranger did not know about what had
happened in Jerusalem. So they said, "The things about Jesus the Naz-
arene, who was a prophet mighty in deed and word in the sight of God
and all the people, and how the chief priests and our rulers delivered
Him to the sentence of death, and crucified Him. But we were hoping
that it was He who was going to redeem Israel" (vv. 19–21). The men
went on to tell Jesus how some women had gone to the tomb early that
morning and found it empty, and how some other disciples had gone to
verify the story (vv. 22–24).

Do you sense the disappointment in these disciples' voices (v. 21)?

Evidently, they didn't think the reports of Jesus' resurrection were really true. Their lack of faith had caused them to either forget or misunderstand the prophetic word concerning the Messiah.

So Jesus began to enlighten them: "'O foolish men and slow of heart to believe in all that the prophets have spoken! Was it not necessary for the Christ to suffer these things and to enter into His glory?' Then beginning with Moses and with all the prophets, He explained to them the things concerning Himself in all the Scriptures" (vv. 25–27).

Thoroughly confused and discouraged because things didn't work out the way they should have, the two disciples concluded God's prophetic plan had backfired. But Jesus Himself came along to clarify the situation. He enlightened these men by using the Old Testament to explain His coming and His ministry.

As they walked, Jesus led the men through the Scriptures to bring them to an understanding of who He is, what was happening, and how they were to perceive the events they had just experienced. In other words, Jesus taught from the Scriptures that prophesied about Him. Even though we do not know exactly what He said to them, we know that everything Jesus taught was about Himself. He is the subject of prophecy.

Revelation 19:10 declares, "The testimony of Jesus is the spirit of prophecy." Studying prophecy is like boarding a spacecraft and orbiting above Earth. You can see things more clearly because you see them at a distance. You get the big picture. Prophecy allows us to see things from a distance of many miles and many years. The wise men are a good example. They saw Jesus' star from a great distance, closed in on it, and found Jesus.

In order for the prophetic Word of God to become real to you, you have to be willing to take the trip. You must be willing to pursue that which God has spoken, because in your pursuit you are exercising faith that what God has said is true. The two disciples from Emmaus had the greatest Teacher teaching from the greatest Book about the greatest person—Himself. And there were only two in the congregation. The problem here was that the men were slow to believe. Later, Jesus said to the group of followers, "Why are you troubled, and why do doubts arise in your hearts?" (Luke 24:38).

If you are going to understand the prophetic Word, you must be willing to give God your heart, not only your head.

The Content of Prophecy

After Jesus revealed Himself to the pair in Emmaus and then vanished, they hurried back to Jerusalem that same night. There they found the apostles and others, and as they were telling their story, Jesus came into the room and conversed with them (Luke 24:28–43). It was time for more teaching. He would summarize prophecy about His life and death. But first He declared, "All things which are written about Me in the Law of Moses and the Prophets and the Psalms must be fulfilled" (v. 44).

The entire Old Testament spoke prophetically of Him, He began. His summary of these prophecies included these facts: "Thus it is written, that the Christ would suffer and rise again from the dead the third day, and that repentance for forgiveness of sins would be proclaimed in His name to all the nations, beginning from Jerusalem" (vv. 46–47).

The death and resurrection of "the Christ," the Messiah, for the forgiveness of sin is the summary and the heart of prophecy. The entire Old Testament can be summed up as looking forward to the coming of the Messiah. This prophecy was given at the beginning of the human race, when God told Satan that the seed would come that would crush Satan's head (Genesis 3:15). The patriarch Israel said this seed would come from the tribe of Judah (Genesis 49:10). And God told David that his throne would endure forever (2 Samuel 7:16) because David would have a greater Son, the Messiah, who would rule and reign. So the Old Testament prophecies concerning Messiah were very specific.

Prophecies of Christ's Birth

Now let's "fast-forward" to the opening chapter of the New Testament, Matthew 1:1–17, the genealogy of Jesus Christ. This is the part most people skip over so they can get to the Christmas story. Big mistake. This genealogy and the one in Luke 3:23–38 are critical to the unfolding of the prophetic story concerning Jesus. They demonstrate that Jesus' claim to be Messiah and King, the ruler from the line of David, was legitimate, because He was the Son of David both legally and biologically.

The Gospels' genealogies form a marvelous testimony to the truth that Jesus is the unique focus and culmination of prophecy. These written records were especially important for the Jews who would come along after Jesus. This is because in AD 70 all of Israel's genealogical records were lost when the Roman army sacked Jerusalem and burned the temple, where the records were stored.

Someone who was claiming to be Messiah, the rightful ruler from the line of David, needed to be able to trace his lineage back to David (2 Samuel 7:12–16), the king whose line would rule forever (v. 16). Therefore, even though the local records were destroyed, God preserved the genealogical records of Jesus in Matthew 1 and Luke 3.

Before we move on to consider the distinct genealogy in Luke, let me point out a seeming problem in Matthew 1:11, which mentions a man named Jeconiah. Remember, for Jesus to have proper claim to the title Messiah, it had to be proven that He was of the line of David. But God had pronounced a curse on Jeconiah, a faithless descendant of David (Jeremiah 22:28–30; "Coniah" in the NASB is the Hebrew of

"Jeconiah"). This curse was that no child—that is, no physical descendant—of Jeconiah would ever succeed sitting on the throne of David. The problem is Joseph was a physical descendant of Jeconiah. Had Jesus been Joseph's biological son, He would have been prevented from sitting on the throne of David by this curse.

However, Jesus was conceived not by Joseph but by the Holy Spirit (Matthew 1:20). Joseph was Jesus' legal father but not His biological father. That's why Matthew 1:16 uses the feminine pronoun to refer to Jesus' birth. Jesus bypassed the curse of Jeconiah and yet retained His legal right to the throne. Satan's attempt to corrupt the messianic line had been thwarted.

The Messiah still needed a biological tie to David, because Old Testament prophecy specified Him as a Son of David. Luke's genealogy (3:23–38) deals with this need, since the lineage of Jesus is traced back to David through "Nathan, the son of David" (v. 31). Jesus' biological tie to David is established through Nathan *by Mary*, His mother.

Luke's account traces Jesus' genealogy all the way back to Adam (v. 38). Why is it important that Jesus be connected to the garden of Eden? Because of the prophecy of the righteous Seed that would come and crush Satan (Genesis 3:15). God is removing all doubt that Jesus is the fulfillment of prophecy.

Matthew traced the genealogy of Jesus through Solomon (Matthew 1:7), while Luke went through Nathan, one of David's sons who never held the throne. With these two genealogies Jesus is shown to be Solomon's legal descendant through Joseph (the Matthew account), with a legitimate claim to the title of Messiah, yet free from the curse of Jeconiah because his earthly father was not his biological father.

The point is that no matter how you trace this thing, Jesus was qualified to declare Himself Israel's Messiah. And any Jew who wanted to verify the record could do so because God preserved Jesus' lineage.

Prophecies of Christ's Death

Not only do the Old Testament prophecies deal with Christ's birth, they foretell His death. One classic passage that describes the Messiah's death for sin is Isaiah 53. Let's consider a few key verses from this chapter. Of the Messiah, Isaiah wrote:

He was despised and forsaken of men, a man of sorrows and acquainted with grief. . . . Surely our griefs He Himself bore, and our sorrows He carried; yet we ourselves esteemed Him stricken, smitten of God, and afflicted. But He was pierced through for our transgressions, He was crushed for our iniquities; the chastening for our well-being fell upon Him, and by His scourging we are healed. (vv. 3–5)

This is a tremendous prophecy of Jesus' death by crucifixion. The apostle Peter, who witnessed the Lord's death, wrote to believers, urging them to bear up under unjust suffering the way Jesus did. Then he added:

You have been called for this purpose, since Christ also suffered for you, leaving you an example for you to follow in His steps, who committed no sin, nor was any deceit found in His mouth; and while being reviled, He did not revile in return; while suffering, He uttered no threats, but kept entrusting Himself to Him who judges righteously; and He Himself bore our sins in His body on the cross, that we might die to sin and live to righteousness; for by His wounds you were healed." (1 Peter 2:21–24)

Compare these two passages, and you'll see the fulfillment of Isaiah 53 in Peter's letter. Peter even quoted Isaiah's reference to Jesus' wounds

(v. 5). Peter also noted that Jesus did not answer His accusers, which is what Isaiah prophesied (v. 7).

Psalm 22 contains another great prophecy that the New Testament applies to Jesus Christ in His death on the cross. The psalm opens with the cry, "My God, my God, why have you forsaken me?" (v. 1), the very cry Jesus would utter from the cross. The psalmist also said, "I am a worm and not a man, a reproach of men and despised by the people. All who see me sneer at me; they separate with the lip, they wag the head, saying, 'Commit yourself to the Lord; let Him deliver him; let Him rescue him, because He delights in him'" (vv. 6–8). This parallels the crucifixion account in Luke 23:35: When Jesus was on the cross, "Even the rulers were sneering at Him, saying, 'He saved others; let Him save Himself if this is the Christ of God.'"

> PSALM 22 OPENS WITH THE VERY CRY JESUS WOULD UTTER FROM THE CROSS.

Descriptions of actual crucifixion—not known in Israel until Roman times—also appear in Psalm 22:

"I am poured out like water, and all my bones are out of joint." (v. 14)

"They pierced my hands and my feet." (v. 16)

"They divide my garments among them, and for my clothing they cast lots." (v. 18)

When a person hung on a cross through crucifixion, the weight of his own body dislocated his joints. Jesus would be pierced through His hands, feet, and side (John 19:34). The soldiers would gamble for His clothing (Matthew 27:35). Jesus' death was clearly prophesied, and He fulfilled every prophecy to the detail.

Prophecies of Christ's Resurrection

Similarly the Old Testament Scriptures predicted the resurrection of the Christ.

In fact, during his Pentecost sermon (Acts 2:14–36), Peter drew on an Old Testament prophecy to prove Jesus was the Messiah (vv. 25–28). The passage Peter quoted was Psalm 16:8–11, in which David wrote: "I have set the Lord continually before me; because He is at my right hand, I will not be shaken. Therefore my heart is glad and my glory rejoices; my flesh also will dwell securely. For You will not abandon my soul to Sheol; nor will You allow Your Holy One to undergo decay" (vv. 8–10).

In Acts 2:29–32 Peter made it clear that the fulfillment of this passage came during the life of Jesus Christ. David had "looked ahead and spoke [prophetically] of the resurrection of the Christ" (v. 31), the Messiah. David wasn't the one resurrected; Jesus was. And, Peter said, "We are all witnesses" (v. 32) to the fact that God raised Christ from the dead.

While alive, Jesus Himself prophesied His own resurrection. He predicted His resurrection on several occasions, both to His disciples (Matthew 17:23; 20:19) and to unbelieving Jews (John 2:18–21). John said that after Jesus was raised, the disciples remembered what He said, and they believed (v. 22).

This is the uniqueness of Christ in prophecy. When you see the many ways that the prophecies about Christ were fulfilled in His first coming, you can have confidence in the prophecies about His second coming and glorious rule (e.g., Daniel 7:14; 1 Peter 1:10–11), and you can have confidence in all that Christ accomplished for you on the cross. With that confidence, you can live boldly the abundant life He died to secure.

Typology about a Coming Messiah

Biblical prophecy and typology are related in the sense that both of them present us with pictures of Christ before He came to earth. Typology is also a study that requires both the Old and New Testaments. That's because the pictures—or types—are the means by which the Old Testament foreshadows the person and work of Christ. Specifically, a type is an Old Testament picture that reveals and points forward to a New Testament truth. The New Testament is the fulfillment of the type, the reality behind the shadow.

Typology and prophecy are related; just as God gave us a prophetic map in Old Testament Scriptures that points us to Jesus, He gave us pictures in the Old Testament that also point to Jesus and remind us of Him. Remember, Christ is the theme of the Old Testament (Matthew 5:17; Luke 24:27, 44; John 5:39). That's what a type is, an Old Testament picture of a New Testament reality.

Many of the Old Testament's ceremonies, regulations, and even people were types of Christ in that they illustrated various aspects of His person and work. Here's an example. When John the Baptist pointed to Jesus and cried out, "Behold, the Lamb of God who takes away the sin of the world!" (John 1:29), John was using an Old Testament type and saying Jesus was the fulfillment of that type. All those sacrificial lambs offered in Israel to cover sin temporarily were a picture of the Lamb who would come and offer His blood to take away sin forever. That's typology.

This is also why we always need to study the whole Bible, by the way.

If you look at the Old Testament without the New Testament, then you don't have the full picture because the Old is fulfilled in the New. But if you have a New Testament without the Old, then you aren't going to understand a lot of what is written in the New, because a large part of the New Testament explains, applies, and fulfills what was written in the Old Testament.

Jesus Himself Points to Typology

This is especially true about Jesus Christ. Jesus was intensely interested in the Old Testament's typology about Himself. Remember how Jesus took the two disciples through the Old Testament and explained what the Scriptures said about Himself (Luke 24:27, 44)? He was talking about typology as well as prophecy.

We can say that because He began with "the Law of Moses" (v. 44), the first five books of the Old Testament, which are full of types of Jesus Christ. The tabernacle in the wilderness was a type of Christ, as was the entire sacrificial system, as we also saw. A lot of the events that happened in the books of Moses typified Jesus (John 3:14–15). Jesus explained His life and ministry using events that happened hundreds of years earlier. He could do this because these things pictured Him, anticipated Him, and pointed forward to Him. That's why Jesus could make this astounding statement: "Do not think that I came to abolish the Law or the Prophets; I did not come to abolish but to fulfill" (Matthew 5:17). Jesus came to bring the Old Testament to its God intended consummation.

Beyond the Shadow to the Real Thing

In Colossians 2:17 Paul said the things of the Old Testament were "a mere shadow of what is to come; but the substance belongs to Christ."

Now, would you rather hug a shadow or a person? There's nothing like the real thing. To embrace the Old Testament alone is to embrace the shadow. To embrace Jesus Christ is to embrace the substance of the shadow, the reality behind the type. To embrace the reality behind typology and show you the uniqueness of Christ, let's turn to the book of Hebrews, a difficult book for many Christians to understand.

Hebrews is often tough to understand because the writer assumes the reader understands the Old Testament. Hebrews is a book about typology—that is, about the fulfillment of the old covenant in Christ. One of the author's favorite words in Hebrews was "better." He uses the word thirteen times to show how the old covenant pointed ahead to something better in Christ.

For example, the writer said Jesus is "much better than the angels, as He has inherited a more excellent name than they" (Hebrews 1:4). Angels remain in vogue, but if you settle for the glory of angels only you settle for second best. Because Jesus is better. Hebrews 7:22 says, "Jesus has become the guarantee of a better covenant."

The Old Testament law was a cumbersome way to live. It involved a complicated system of rituals and sacrifices. Jesus is a better way than the old covenant. Besides, according to Hebrews 7:19, "the Law made nothing perfect." But Jesus introduced "a better hope," something we can hold on to and be confident in as we approach God. Because the old covenant had become useless (see 7:18) in justifying sinners before God, it was necessary for a better sacrifice to be offered (9:23). This was the sacrifice Jesus made on the cross.

If you and I were living under the Old Testament, we'd have to bring to the temple a lamb or a goat or some other sacrifice, which would be killed and its blood offered to cover sin. But the good news of the gospel is that the final sacrifice for sin has already been made. Thanks to what Christ has done for us, we can also look forward to "a better country, that is, a heavenly one." God has prepared a city called heaven for us (Hebrews 11:16). The promised land of Canaan was a type of heaven, but the Israelites' best day in Canaan cannot begin to compare with what Jesus has prepared for us (John 14:1–3). We have a better home.

Old Testament Sacrifices—
All Pictures of the Coming Jesus

The Israelites offered five basic kinds of sacrifices under the Law. They were the burnt offering, the grain offering, the peace offering, the sin offering, and the trespass offering. The first three offerings had to do with dedication to God, while the last two had to do with atonement for sin. But Jesus Christ is pictured in all the sacrifices. Jesus fulfilled the type represented by the first three sacrifices through His life of total submission and complete obedience to God the Father. Jesus' declaration on earth was, "Behold, I have come (in the scroll of the book it is written of Me) to do Your will, O God" (Hebrews 10:7).

If Jesus had disobeyed God even once, He would have been disqualified from being our Savior. But once again, He is unique among all people—He obeyed God perfectly. The sin offering and trespass offering were fulfilled by Christ's death.

The study of the tabernacle as a type of Christ is worth a book in itself. God specified in the book of Exodus how He wanted this place built, and every detail pointed ahead to Christ in some fashion. Before the temple was built, the tabernacle was the dwelling place of God, the location of His Shekinah, His glory. If you wanted to hang out with God, you had to hang out in the tabernacle. But with Jesus' sacrifice, direct access would be possible. Here are just a few of the ways Jesus fulfilled the type of the tabernacle:

- There was one door in the tabernacle. Jesus said He was the way (John 14:6).

- The tabernacle contained a brass altar for sacrifice. Jesus said in Mark 10:45 that He came to give His life as a ransom or sacrifice for many.

- The tabernacle also contained a light, and we know that Jesus said, "I am the Light of the world" (John 8:12).

- Also in the tabernacle was a table on which sat some consecrated bread. Jesus called Himself "the bread of life" (John 6:48).

- The high priest burned incense in the tabernacle to symbolize the prayers that went up to God. Jesus acted as our High Priest when He prayed for us (John 17:9).

- A veil hung in the tabernacle to separate the outer chambers from the inner part, the Holy of Holies. It signified that full access to God was not yet achieved. But when Jesus died, the veil in the temple was torn in half (Matthew 27:51). The writer of Hebrews said the veil was Christ's body (Hebrews 10:20).

- In the Holy of Holies resided the ark of God with its covering called the mercy seat, where the blood of the sacrificial lamb was sprinkled to atone for sin. Jesus said in John 10:15, "I lay down My life."

Do you get the idea? The tabernacle, which was a tent, housed the presence and glory of God. When Jesus came, the Bible says, "The Word became flesh, and dwelt [literally, 'tabernacled'] among us, and we saw His glory" (John 1:14). The word "dwelt" meant to pitch a tent, like the tabernacle. The connection between Christ and the tabernacle could not be clearer. The purpose of the tabernacle was to display God's glory, and when Jesus came people could see God's glory in Him. Jesus uniquely and perfectly fulfilled this type as well.

Another type, or shadow, of the Jesus to come is the rock. When Israel was wandering in the desert, the people became hungry and thirsty. So Moses struck a rock, and enough water gushed out to water the entire nation (Numbers 20:11). That wasn't just a rock. It was a type of Christ. The apostle Paul explained this typology to the Corinthians, "[They] all drank the same spiritual drink, for they were drinking from a spiritual rock which followed them; and the rock was Christ" (1 Corinthians 10:4). That was the spiritual provision of God through the second person of the Trinity. If Christ was sufficient for Israel in the wilderness, He can get you through your desert. He can give you water to drink and become your satisfaction.

> THAT WASN'T JUST A ROCK. IT WAS A TYPE OF CHRIST.

The Israelites also needed manna to eat in the wilderness (Exodus 16:14–15). Jesus told the Jews, "I am the bread that came down out of heaven" (John 6:41). The manna was a picture, a type, that pointed forward to Jesus, the true Bread of Life that would come down from heaven and nourish us.

In John 3:14–15, Jesus said, "As Moses lifted up the serpent in the wilderness, even so must the Son of Man be lifted up; so that whoever believes will in Him have eternal life." Jesus was referring to a severe judgment God sent on Israel for disobedience, in which the people were being bitten by poisonous snakes (Numbers 21:4–9). God told Moses to make a bronze serpent and put it up on a pole, so that anyone who looked at the serpent on the pole would live. Jesus said this figure was a type of the sacrifice He would make for sins. Being lifted up here does not mean lifting Jesus up in praise or adoration. It referred to His being lifted up on the cross—just as the bronze serpent was lifted up for deliverance from death.

Looking at the serpent required an act of faith, just as believing that Jesus' death on the cross will save you requires an act of faith. Some Israelites may have refused to look up at the serpent, looking around instead for a doctor. But whoever refused to look died! Jesus says, "Look to Me and live."

Jesus is the Lamb of God prophesied to come. He is also the perfect fulfillment of every Old Testament type, the reality behind all the pictures. And just as the twenty-six letters of the English alphabet are all we will ever need for any word in the English language, Jesus Christ and His death on the cross and subsequent resurrection are all we need for any situation or circumstance life may bring our way.

3

THE DEATH

ALMOST EVERY TIME a healthy baby is born, the parents, attending doctor, and assisting nurse will smile at the beauty of the newborn. The infant may cry at first, but the innocence of the new life will bring joy to all.

The parents may recognize in their baby their own physical features within the day or month. But they may be unaware of the truth: They also pass on to that baby their sin nature, just as surely as the parents transmit their hair and eye color and other traits. The reality is our child is no less innocent than we are. Sin awaits each of us.

Scripture tells us, "Through one man sin entered into the world, and death through sin, and so death spread to all men, because all sinned" (Romans 5:12). Sin entered the world through Adam, the first of the human race. His human nature, and Eve's too, were contaminated through sin, and they passed the contamination on through the procreation of the race.

The doctrine Paul is teaching here is called *imputation*, a fancy word for crediting something to a person's account. Adam's sin was charged to the account of his offspring, the human race. You, me, our children, and all of humanity.

This teaching has been the subject of a lot of theological debate. But

Paul says all of us have sinned, so don't worry about whether you are going to have to pay for Adam's sin. We have our own sin to deal with. Sin's contamination is universal.

The biblical writers are frank. David writes, "I was brought forth in iniquity, and in sin my mother conceived me" (Psalm 51:5). Paul wrote of himself, "I know that nothing good dwells in me, that is, in my flesh; for the willing is present in me, but the doing of the good is not" (Romans 7:18).

The final result of sin's contamination is death. We usually think of physical death, but actually the Bible teaches three kinds of death. There is physical death, the separation of the body from the soul and spirit; spiritual death, in which a person is separated from fellowship with God; and eternal death, in which a person is separated from God forever. Notice that the key element is always separation.

> JESUS CHRIST HAD TO DIE BECAUSE NOTHING SHORT OF HIS DEATH COULD ERADICATE PERVASIVE SIN.

This is why Jesus Christ had to die, because sin is so pervasive and so corrupting that nothing short of His death could eradicate it. At the heart of sin is the desire to be independent of God, to do things our own way. Our human desire for independence from God is a reaction of rebellion. We don't want to be answerable to Him. The Bible describes this attitude in Romans 1, which we will look at more deeply in a later chapter, "Even though they [unbelievers] knew God, they did not honor Him as God or give thanks, but they became futile in their speculations, and their foolish heart was darkened. . . . Just as they did not see fit to acknowledge God any longer, God gave them over to a depraved mind, to do those things which are not proper" (vv. 21, 28).

Independence says, "I don't want to honor God. I want to do my thing. I want to be my own boss." This attitude actually originated in heaven—in the heart and mind of the angel Lucifer, who said, "I will make myself like the Most High" (Isaiah 14:14). Any attempt on our part to be independent of God is an expression of sin. And, like Satan, who was cast out of heaven (Isaiah 14:12–15; Luke 10:18), we are kept from heaven until we acknowledge our sin and accept Jesus' sacrifice that removes sin's penalty.

The Standard That Defines Sin

Romans 3:23 declares the standard by which sin is measured: "the glory of God." In other words, when God measures this problem called sin, He measures it against Himself, not your neighbor or the person at work. God doesn't say, "You are a pretty good person"; He says, "You are not as good as I."

Most non-Christians either don't understand or don't believe that, so they don't think sin is a big deal. They don't see why someone has to die to answer for sin. They think God judges using scales to weigh our good deeds against our bad deeds, or else He grades on the curve. But the Bible says everyone falls short—we fail to measure up to the standard, because the standard is God's perfection. Who can measure up to that ultimate standard? No one!

Imagine two travelers missing their flight at the airport. One traveler misses the flight by just five seconds, while the other person is forty-five minutes late. Is the first person any better off? No, it's irrelevant how far short of the standard the two people fell. They are both stuck at the airport.

In the same way, we have fallen short of heaven, and it doesn't matter whether we miss heaven by an inch or a mile. God must respond to sin because His controlling attribute is holiness.

The prophet Habakkuk said, "Your eyes are too pure to approve evil, and You can not look on wickedness with favor" (1:13). When even righteous people in the Bible came face-to-face with God's holiness, they weren't casual about it. Isaiah, like Habakkuk an obedient prophet, still cried out in the presence of a holy God, "Woe is me, for I am ruined!" (Isaiah 6:5), a word that means he was coming apart at the seams.

Job—not a prophet yet a godly man who had been commended by God (Job 1:8)—met an awesome God after his testing and realized his sinfulness: "Now my eye sees You; therefore I retract, and I repent in dust and ashes" (Job 42:5b–6). Stand in Job's or Isaiah's sandals for a minute, and you'll understand why Jesus had to die for sin and why no one else but Jesus could make that payment.

Since God is the offended party when we sin, it is His prerogative to determine on what basis sin shall be atoned for and forgiven. That basis is clearly spelled out in Hebrews 9:22: "According to the Law, one may almost say, all things are cleansed with blood, and without shedding of blood there is no forgiveness."

A Blood Sacrifice

The means by which God forgives sin is the shedding of blood. Anything less than that doesn't get the job done. All of the moaning and groaning and promising to turn over new leaves that people do will not remove sin. Sin is a capital offense. It carries the death penalty. Why did God decree that blood was the required payment for sin? Because the shedding of blood requires death, since "the life of the flesh is in the blood" (Leviticus 17:11).

The requirement of blood to deal with sin goes all the way back to Eden, when God killed an animal to cover Adam and Eve after they sinned (Genesis 3:21). The animal's death satisfied God's requirement and substituted for their deaths. Christ's death was, therefore, a blood atonement. He offered Himself as a sacrificial substitution for the death our sins deserved.

The apostle Peter, who was present at Jesus' crucifixion, made this great statement: "He Himself bore our sins in His body on the cross" (1 Peter 2:24). Why did Jesus have to die on the cross? The Bible explains why, and when you see it you'll be grateful for the cross. The Bible says, "Christ redeemed us from the curse of the Law, having become a curse for us—for it is written, 'Cursed is everyone who hangs on a tree'" (Galatians 3:13). Notice that the Law of Moses had a curse attached to it. Just three verses earlier Paul had written, quoting Deuteronomy 27:26, "Cursed is everyone who does not abide by all things written in the book of the law, to perform them" (Galatians 3:10).

So if you failed in one point of the Law, you blew the whole thing and came under the Law's curse (James 2:10). That's very bad, but here's something very good. Jesus took our curse for us by hanging on a tree, another term for the cross. To demonstrate his point, Paul quoted Deuteronomy 21:23, which pronounced a curse on anyone who hung on a tree.

In Old Testament days, a person who committed a capital crime would be executed, usually by stoning. If the crime was particularly hideous, the dead criminal would then be hung from a tree as the ultimate form of disgrace and shame. This also served as a warning to others, as you can imagine. This was not crucifixion, but the central idea was to bring shame to the criminal. It was obvious to all that a person hung on a tree was cursed.

So why death on a cross for Jesus? Because God wanted to demonstrate to the world that Jesus was bearing the curse of the Law for us. Jesus hung on a tree as an object of open shame so it would be clear beyond any doubt that God was allowing the deathblow of His curse to fall on His Son. All so that you and I could go free.

The good news is that God accepted Christ's death as payment in full for our sins (see John 19:30). God now would no longer impute, or charge, our sins against our account (2 Corinthians 5:19). How could God not do that? Because "He [God the Father] made Him who knew no sin to be sin on our behalf, that we might become the righteousness of God in Him" (v. 21). God charged our sins to Jesus' account and credited Jesus' perfect righteousness to our account. The death of Christ allows God to grant sinful men a perfect credit score.

The Motive

So why would God willingly send His Son to the cross and why would Jesus willingly die? If anything sets Jesus Christ apart from all others and makes Him unique, it is His love for sinners like us. He loves people, unworthy as they are. Similarly the Father loved us and sent the perfect redeemer, His Son. Think about it. Would you offer to sacrifice your child for a rebel, a scoundrel? That may sound harsh, but that's who every man and woman is and that is what God did for us in Christ.

We were not a pretty sight to God, but He loved us even at our worst. "While we were yet sinners" (Romans 5:8) when Christ went to the cross. That's why if you don't understand the cross, you will never fully understand love. God's love is His joyful self-determination to reflect His goodness and glory by meeting the needs of mankind.

That's a big definition, so let me put it in everyday terms. God's love is always *visible*: God so loved that He gave His Son (John 3:16). God's love is also *sacrificial*. He loved to the point of paying a price for us. God's love is also unconditional. He had His Son die for us before we got our act cleaned up, "while we were yet sinners" (Romans 5:8). In fact,

God doesn't want you cleaning up your own act, because you are going to miss some spots. He didn't put any conditions on His love.

Jesus died for us when we were sinners. What's more is that He did it both willingly and in all humiliation.

The Humiliation of the Cross

The word "humiliation" is a theological term that describes the steps downward Jesus Christ took in leaving the highest position in heaven for the lowest position on earth. The implications of Jesus' humiliation in coming to earth and dying on the cross are staggering. For a basic understanding of this great truth, we can study Philippians 2:5–11, which offers crucial details of Christ's humiliation.

We can only begin to appreciate how far down Jesus came when we realize how exalted He is. Scripture tells us Jesus "existed in the form of God" (2:6). There never has been a time when Jesus did not exist as God. The word "form" means inner essence or being. Hebrews 13:8 says Jesus Christ is the same yesterday, today, and forever. Who Jesus is today, He always has been.

Yet this One who was and is fully God "did not regard equality with God a thing to be grasped" (2:6). He did not hold on selfishly to all the glory and delights of heaven. Even though we will never understand completely what all this means, we need to come to grips with what Jesus did, because only when we reflect the image of Christ on the cross in our own thoughts and attitudes will we be positioned to fully experience all of its benefits and blessings.

One thing we know is that Jesus was not insecure about letting go of the privileges of Deity. It's not as if someone else was going to usurp His place in heaven. Jesus had nothing to worry about there. Jesus also did not need to hold on to His privileged position in heaven to maintain

His position, because none of His deity was diminished, compromised, or impaired in the slightest when He became a man. Whatever the humiliation and self-emptying of Jesus means, it does not mean He laid aside His deity.

The reason Jesus was willing to leave heaven and take on human form is because of the mindset He had. He did not object to giving up His prerogatives for the greater good and glory of God. Jesus could have said, "I don't want to be nailed to a tree to pay for the sins of those rebels." He could have said, "Send someone else." But in eternity past, Jesus Christ made a decision to act on our behalf. No wonder John said, "We love, because He first loved us" (1 John 4:19).

Philippians 2:7 gets to the heart of what it meant for Christ to humble Himself. This is a somewhat controversial passage, because there are differences of opinion over what is included in Christ's "emptying," or *kenosis* (the Greek term). The text says Christ "emptied Himself, taking the form of a bond-servant, and being made in the likeness of men." Verses 6 and 7 describe the extent of Christ's humiliation: He was "in the form of God," but on earth He assumed "the form of a bond-servant," a slave. Paul's use of this term is important. Why didn't he just say Jesus took on the form of a human being? That would be humiliation enough for God. There's a Greek word for humanity in general Paul could have used here, or he could have used the word that meant a male as opposed to a female. But Paul used neither of these. Instead, he chose the more specific Greek word *doulos*, which means "slave."

> JESUS BECAME A SLAVE. SO HE CAN IDENTIFY WITH YOU IN ANY SITUATION: POVERTY, LONELINESS, HOMELESSNESS, REJECTION.

In other words, Jesus became a particular kind of man—a slave, the lowest position within the Roman world. This is good news for you. No matter how low you may get, you can never sink so far that Jesus cannot get under you and lift you up. He can identify with you in any situation, no matter how hard: poverty, loneliness, homelessness, rejection, you name it.

Philippians 2:7 adds that Jesus was "made in the likeness of men." That means He looked like an ordinary man. He didn't go around with a halo around His head, nor did He float above the ground. Jesus Himself said He came not to be served—which was His right and prerogative as God—but to serve, which is what a slave does (Mark 10:45). A slave doesn't have any rights. So when Jesus took on a human body, He also volunteered to accept the limitations of being human.

He lived as a man without using His deity for His personal benefit or to avoid having to face the hardships and temptations of everyday human life. In other words, Jesus did not use His divine power to solve a problem for His humanity. One example of this is in His temptation, when He was hungry and the devil tempted Him to turn stones into bread (Matthew 4:3). But the greatest example is in the garden of Gethsemane, when Jesus rebuked Peter for drawing his sword and accepted His arrest.

Now don't misunderstand. Jesus did use His divine power on many occasions. We call those occasions miracles. But the miracles were always done for the benefit of the kingdom and the blessing of others, not to make Jesus' life easier. The reason He forsook using His deity was that He might experience every pain and temptation we face (Hebrews 4:15) so He could reverse the first Adam's failure and win the spiritual battle Adam lost for mankind in Eden. Jesus lived out the will of God on earth that He might be an acceptable substitute for man.

The Humility of Emptying

When we take a look at Philippians 2:8, we discover that Jesus took on human flesh and became a bond-servant for a very specific purpose: "Being found in appearance as a man, He humbled Himself by becoming obedient to the point of death, even death on a cross." Jesus came for the cross.

Yet in His humanity there was a struggle. Remember His prayer in Gethsemane? "My Father, if it is possible, let this cup pass from Me" (Matthew 26:39).

How difficult was it for Jesus to face the cross? So difficult an angel had to strengthen Him in the garden of Gethsemane as He bore the agony of it (Luke 22:43–44).

But in that same garden, after asking that the cross might be lifted from Him, Jesus prayed, "Yet not what I will, but what You will" (Mark 14:36). We are to have the same attitude in ourselves. Jesus did not have to go to the cross. But when He came to the greatest crisis of His life, He submitted Himself to God's will and was obedient to death because of His love for us.

The Humble Mediator

Another aspect of the purpose behind Jesus Christ's humiliation and self-emptying is this: It put Him in position to be the mediator we need. In 1 Timothy 2, after Paul urged Christians to pray for everyone, he said, "There is one God, and one mediator also between God and men, the man Christ Jesus, who gave Himself as a ransom for all" (vv. 5–6). A mediator is a go-between, someone who can stand between two parties who are at odds with each other and bring them together. The humble Jesus is the mediator between God and us.

On the cross, Jesus literally hung between two estranged parties, His Father and the human race, to bring us to God. The concept of a mediator is an old one. In Job, considered the oldest book of the Bible, the patriarch sensed his need for a go-between so he could plead his case before God. Job was struggling and hurting, as we know. He was desperate for help as his three friends accused him of sin. At one point, Job said, "How can a man be in the right before God? If one wished to dispute with Him, he could not answer Him once in a thousand times" (Job 9:2–3). How can a human argue with God? That's what Job was asking.

Job recognized his dilemma. God "is not a man as I am that I may answer Him, that we may go to court together. There is no umpire between us, who may lay his hand upon us both" (vv. 32–33). Job wanted a go-between, or "umpire." This is the same principle as a mediator, one who arbitrates between two parties. In order to be an effective mediator between a perfect, holy God and sinners, someone would have to know how God feels and thinks—someone like God, in other words. And this mediator would have to know how we think and feel—someone like us. Jesus Christ uniquely fulfills that requirement. That's why the Bible says He is the one Mediator who can stand between God and us.

In Philippians 2:9–11, Paul wrote, "For this reason also, God highly exalted Him, and bestowed on Him the name which is above every name, so that at the name of Jesus every knee will bow, of those who are in heaven and on earth and under the earth, and that every tongue will confess that Jesus Christ is Lord, to the glory of God the Father."

Jesus' humiliation is not the end of the story. God raised Jesus up from the grave of His humanity and exalted Him in heaven as the God-man. When you and I meet Jesus in heaven, we will not see the pre-incarnate Jesus. We will see the resurrected Jesus, the God-man. Through His willingness to humble Himself to the point of death, even death on the cross. Jesus Christ is exalted above everyone and everything in the universe.

4

THE RESURRECTION AND ASCENSION

THROUGH ANCIENT AND modern history, there have been many teachers and religious leaders—some great, some near great, and some not so great. On some pundits' lists you might find the Greek philosophers Socrates (who developed the Socratic method of teaching by asking questions) and his protégé Plato. Some would include English philosopher and teacher John Locke. Students in the East would cite Confucius or Siddhartha Gautama, better known as Buddha (literally "the enlightened one").

These leaders taught various worldviews and philosophies, and many of them acquired great followings. Some even died for their cause, which sometimes made them seem larger than life.

But there is a dramatic difference between all of these leaders and Jesus Christ. Despite the claims of some to represent God, or even to be God Himself, these other leaders are dead, buried, and gone. Jesus Christ had an earthly death too. But there the difference ends. Jesus Christ stepped out of His grave on the third day.

Without the resurrection, Christianity would have been stillborn. You can't have a living faith if all you have is a dead savior. Without the resurrection, the Christian faith might be a commendable way of life, but Jesus would be just another great teacher who lived His life and returned to dust. Christianity would not be the truth from God if Jesus did not rise from the dead. His resurrection makes Jesus Christ unique.

Other religions can compete with Christianity on some things. They can say, for example, "Your founder gave you a holy book? Our founder gave us a holy book. Your founder has a large following? So does ours. You have buildings where people come to worship your God? We have buildings where people come to worship our god." But only Christians can say, "All of that may be true, but our Founder rose from the dead!" That's the uniqueness of the resurrection.

In this final chapter looking at the person of the cross, I want to talk about the validity, the value, and the victory of Christ's resurrection.

The Resurrection's Validity

We confidently believe and teach that George Washington and Patrick Henry existed because we have reliable, written documentation of their lives. No one alive today has seen George Washington in the flesh. None of us was present when America won its independence from Britain. But we accept these people and events as true because of the reliability of the documentation.

The same argument holds true for Jesus Christ. The documentation validates His resurrection. Let me give you a number of proofs that validate the resurrection.

The first proof of Jesus' resurrection is *His empty tomb*. This is a huge problem for those who doubt and reject the resurrection. The issue is simple. If Jesus died and stayed dead, then why did His tomb turn up empty?

Christianity could have been stopped before it got started if Jesus' enemies had simply produced His dead body. After all, they were the ones who had control over the tomb.

"Oh," some people say, "that's easy to explain. Any number of things could have happened to the body." Several theories are put forth to explain the empty tomb of Jesus. One of these is the so-called swoon theory. This argues that Jesus did not die on the cross but simply lapsed into deep unconsciousness. Since the people of that day were medically unsophisticated, they assumed Jesus was dead and buried Him. But the coolness of the tomb revived Jesus. He got up, shook off the effects of all His horrible injuries, unwrapped His grave clothes, pushed aside the stone without disturbing the Roman guards, and snuck away, then re-appeared to claim He had been raised from the dead.

The best argument against this theory is the action of Jesus' enemies themselves. They made sure He was dead. When the Roman soldiers came to finish off the men on the crosses, they saw that Jesus was al-ready dead. But just to make sure, "one of the soldiers pierced His side with a spear, and immediately blood and water came out" (John 19:34). When Pilate heard Jesus was dead, he checked with the centurion to make sure (Mark 15:44–45).

Another theory is that the disciples went to the wrong tomb when they re-ported that Jesus was alive, because it was dark and they were confused and upset. But even if that happened, all the Jews and Pilate had to do was take the disciples to the right tomb and show them Jesus' body.

> TO STEAL JESUS' BODY, ELEVEN CIVILIAN DISCIPLES WOULD HAVE HAD TO OVERPOWER A WELL-ARMED DETAIL OF UP TO SIXTEEN ROMAN SOLDIERS.

A third theory that was popular for a while was the idea that the disciples stole Jesus' body and then claimed His resurrection. But this theory ignores all the precautions that Pilate took to make sure that did not happen. The Jews feared that very thing, so they went to Pilate and said, "Sir, we remember that when He was still alive that deceiver said, 'After three days I am to rise again.' Therefore, give orders for the grave to be made secure until the third day, otherwise His disciples may come and steal Him away and say to the people, 'He has risen from the dead'" (Matthew 27:63–64). So Pilate gave them a Roman detail to guard the tomb and permission to seal the tomb with a Roman seal (vv. 65–66).

To steal Jesus' body, eleven civilian disciples would have had to overpower a well-armed detail of up to sixteen Roman soldiers and remove a stone that weighed more than a ton to get to Jesus. But more than that, the disciples would have had to break that official Roman seal, which was an offense punishable by death. Besides, where could they have hidden a dead body so no one would detect it? And if they did pull a deception like that, why would the disciples then go out and give their lives for what they knew was a lie?

The Witness of the Grave Clothes

When John first arrived at Jesus' tomb and looked in, he saw "the linen wrappings lying there, and the face-cloth which had been on His head, not lying with the linen wrappings, but rolled up in a place by itself" (John 20:6–7). That was enough for John to believe in Jesus' resurrection. The reason is the way the grave clothes were arranged.

In biblical days corpses were wrapped with one cloth around the body and a different piece of cloth around the head. The cloths were wound around the body and the head so that the headpiece was like a turban. Then the body was laid faceup on a shelf in the tomb. What John described was a scene in which the grave clothes were lying undisturbed. The headpiece was not unwound but still wrapped and lying in a separate place from the other wrappings. The only way these grave clothes could still be in position with no body in them is if Jesus came right through them. If He had not died, but revived and escaped as some say, He would have had to unwrap to get out. The clothes would have been piled in a heap on the floor of the tomb. But Jesus came through those grave clothes in His resurrected, glorified body.

The Witness of the Disciples' Transformed Lives

Another "convincing proof" that validates the resurrection is *the transformation that took place in the lives of the disciples.* Peter denied he knew Jesus three times at the crucifixion. But just a few weeks later, Peter "taking his stand with the eleven, raised his voice and declared" the gospel fearlessly on the day of Pentecost (Acts 2:14). It took a lot of courage for Peter to declare, "This Man . . . you nailed to a cross by the hands of godless men and put Him to death. But God raised Him up again" (vv. 23–24). It's not likely he would put himself in jeopardy like that for a lie.

A couple of chapters later in Acts, Peter and the apostles were getting beaten for their message. James lost his life, and Peter wound up in jail under a death sentence (Acts 12). Saul was present at the stoning of Stephen, giving his approval (Acts 7:58; 8:1). He was determined to eradicate this new sect called Christians. And he was good at it too (Philippians 3:6). Yet this hostile witness later would testify (1 Corinthians 15:8) that he had seen the risen Jesus on the Damascus road (Acts 9:5).

After meeting the risen Christ, Saul was never the same. He became the apostle Paul, who would become so convinced of the truth of the resurrection that he would put his life on the line for it, when his former Jewish pals tried to kill him for becoming a Christian.

The Value of the Resurrection

The resurrection of Jesus Christ is not only validated; it is incredibly valuable. I want to mention just two key benefits of Jesus' empty tomb: (1) the Bible is shown to be reliable and (2) our salvation is assured. Since the Old Testament prophesied Jesus' resurrection (Psalm 16:10; cf. Acts 13:34–35), the Bible is validated as the inerrant revelation of God. The New Testament Gospels reveal that Jesus personally prophesied His resurrection on several occasions. "From that time Jesus began to show His disciples that He must go to Jerusalem, and suffer many things from the elders and chief priests and scribes, and be killed, and be raised up on the third day" (Matthew 16:21; cf. Mark 8:31; Luke 9:22).

Later, Jesus told the disciples they were going to Jerusalem, where He would be delivered to the Gentiles, who, He said, would "mock and scourge and crucify Him, and on the third day He [would] be raised up" (Matthew 20:18–19). Then on resurrection day, an angel at the tomb would tell Mary Magdalene, "He is not here, for He has risen, just as He said" (Matthew 28:6). If Jesus were wrong about His resurrection, then we should not believe anything else He said. If He did rise from the dead, then we can believe everything else He said.

Jesus' resurrection also confirms our salvation. It is the divine guarantee, God's "receipt," showing that Jesus' death satisfied the payment demanded for sin. Paul said in Romans 4:25 that Jesus was delivered to the cross for our sins and "was raised because of our justification." When He cried, "It is finished!" on the cross (John 19:30), He was announcing that the price for sin had been paid in full. Therefore, if you have received Jesus Christ as your Savior by faith, His resurrection is your guarantee that your salvation is secure.

In his Pentecost sermon, Peter said of Jesus, "God raised Him up again, putting an end to the agony of death, since it was impossible for Him to be held in its power" (Acts 2:24). Death was unable to hold Christ, not only because He is God but because His death broke the power of sin. Sin is the only power that can hold

> JESUS' RESURRECTION IS GOD'S "RECEIPT," SHOWING THAT JESUS' DEATH SATISFIED THE PAYMENT DEMANDED FOR SIN.

a person in death. Death only exists because of sin, so when sin is done away with, death has lost its hold on us (1 Corinthians 15:55–56).

We have seen the validity and the value of Christ's resurrection. But by His walking out of the tomb, He also offers us personal victory.

Victory over Sin's Power

In His resurrection, Jesus gave us victory over sin—both now and in the future, when the grave has to let go of us. On our resurrection day we will be free from the very presence of sin because we will be in heaven.

But Christ's resurrection does gives us victory over sin in the here and now. That's what Paul said in Romans 6:1–5, a crucial passage in which he explained that when we accepted Christ we were identified completely with Him, both in His death and in His resurrection. So when Christ was raised from the dead, you also were raised to a new way of life. We need this new connection to Christ because of our old connection to Adam. When Adam sinned, his death sentence was passed on to all of us, as we learned earlier, because all of us have sinned. So our connection to Adam brought death, and death is a reality for all of us. But when we believe in Jesus, we get connected to Him. And when we get connected to Jesus, we get connected to His resurrection life in the same way we were plugged into death through Adam.

Therefore, if you and I have sin in our lives that is overcoming us and beating us down, it is because we have adopted faulty thinking. We are living as if Christ's resurrection life within us is theoretical and not real. The analogy is this: If death is real and not just theoretical, then your new life in Christ and your new power over sin are real and not theoretical. If you will learn to identify with your new life in Christ (Ephesians 2:5), rather than with your old life in Adam, you will have new victory in Christ rather than old defeat in Adam.

You and I need to learn to think in terms of, "I am not what I used to be, so I don't have to act like I used to act." Some of us have it backward. We say, "Okay, I'm going to stop doing this." So we take a deep breath and give it our best shot. We make all the resolutions, but in a few days or weeks we're back where we started. Self-effort is not the answer. If it were, you could have stopped a long time ago.

What's needed is to say to God, "I can't do it. I can't stop. I can't help myself. But here and now, I thank You that You have already given me the victory over this in Christ. I thank You that because He rose from the dead, You have given me the strength I need to live above this sin. So by faith, I am going to walk in the victory You gave me—and not in the old defeat I have when I try it on my own." That's the only way you can tap into resurrection power that is yours in Christ.

When Jesus said, "Apart from Me you can do nothing" (John 15:5), that's just what He meant. When you connect yourself to Christ as a daily reality, you experience His resurrection power and His victory over sin. That's the key, because the Christian life is "Christ in you, the hope of glory" (Colossians 1:27).

Even More Victory through Jesus' Ascension

Every four years the US government stages the closest thing the country has to the coronation of a king or queen—the inauguration of a president. Government officials gather in Washington, DC, for the ceremony, while most of its citizens watch on television this bestowing of authority. The inauguration is the moment when the new or returning president is publicly recognized as the leader of the nation.

A presidential inauguration is impressive. But none of these events can begin to compare with the enthronement of Jesus Christ at the right hand of God, the coronation with which He was honored when He ascended back to heaven after His resurrection.

The first thing to understand about the ascension after the cross is its importance. Jesus' return in a cloud to heaven is an important confirmation of the truth of Scripture, and it has staggering implications for us today. In his great sermon to the Jews on the day of Pentecost, the apostle Peter said,

This Jesus God raised up again, to which we are all witnesses. Therefore having been exalted to the right hand of God, and having received from the Father the promise of the Holy Spirit, He has poured forth this which you both see and hear. For it was not David who ascended into heaven, but he himself says: "The Lord said to my Lord, 'Sit at My right hand, until I make Your enemies a footstool for Your feet.'" (Acts 2:32–35)

Peter's quotation is from Psalm 110:1, a prophecy made almost one thousand years before Jesus was born. David looked ahead and prophesied that Christ would ascend to God and be seated at His right hand.

77

So the ascension is another important validation of God's prophetic Word in the Old Testament.

Acts 1:9 says Jesus "was lifted up," and that "a cloud received Him." He was departing in the cloud. Two angels said He was "taken up" (v. 11). In other words, Jesus' ascension was gradual, visible, and physical. This was not a mirage, not a trick or the result of any sleight of hand. In the same way that Jesus arose bodily, He ascended bodily. The Bible prophesied His ascension, and in the presence of His disciples, Jesus ascended back to heaven.

The ascension and present ministry of Jesus are all-important for you and me as we seek to live the dynamic, victorious, Spirit-filled Christian life that is God's will for us. During the Last Supper, after predicting His ascension, Jesus told the disciples, "I tell you the truth, it is to your advantage that I go away; for if I do not go away, the Helper will not come to you; but if I go, I will send Him to you" (John 16:7). This, of course, is Jesus' promise to send the Holy Spirit, of whom Jesus had said, "He abides with you and will be in you" (John 14:17). Jesus said His ascension would initiate the ministry of the Holy Spirit and that this would be even better for the disciples than His physical presence.

How can this be? Because when Jesus was on earth, He functioned in one location at a time. So when someone needed Jesus to meet a serious need, as happened on several occasions, He had to leave where He was and go with the person who needed Him. But because the Holy Spirit lives within each believer, He goes with us wherever we go. And He is always present in full power with each believer in the world, all at the same time.

The Holy Spirit is not subject to the limitations of human flesh to which Jesus voluntarily submitted so He could be our Savior. That's part of the good news of Jesus' ascension.

Jesus' ascension is also at the heart of one of the most precious promises in the Bible. The night before His death, Jesus assured His followers, "In My Father's house are many dwelling places; if it were not so, I would have told you; for I go to prepare a place for you. If I go and

> IF THE ASCENSION IS TRUE, THEN HEAVEN IS TRUE.

prepare a place for you, I will come again, and receive you to Myself; that where I am, there you may be also" (John 14:2–3). The ascension is vital to our hope for tomorrow and for eternity. Jesus not only ascended to return to His Father and send us the promised Holy Spirit but to prepare heaven for our occupancy someday. Because Jesus went somewhere, we have somewhere to go. And just as Christ ascended to heaven, you and I will leave this earth someday and ascend to heaven because Jesus is coming back for us. If the ascension is true, then heaven is true.

The Accomplishments of the Ascension

The second aspect of Christ's ascension is its accomplishments. What is true today because Jesus ascended to the Father? When Jesus ascended, He was enthroned at God's right hand and every power in the universe was made subject to Him—particularly the spirit realm, both the holy angels and the demonic world.

Peter wrote that Christ is "at the right hand of God, having gone into heaven, after angels and authorities and powers had been subjected to Him" (1 Peter 3:22). The writer of Hebrews also established the authority of the risen and ascended Christ: "When He had made purification of sins, He sat down at the right hand of the Majesty on high, having become as much better than the angels, as He has inherited a more excellent name than they" (Hebrews 1:3–4). Christ was exalted over the angelic realm in His ascension, and that has huge implications for you and me.

That brings us to the ascension's second great accomplishment. Paul said that because of our identification with Christ, we are raised up with Him and "seated . . . with Him in the heavenly places" (Ephesians 2:6). We are rulers in the heavenly realm with Christ! In His ascension, redeemed mankind was elevated to a position of authority over the angelic world.

The ascension of Jesus, and our identification with Him, *gives us tremendous authority for service to Him.* Just before His ascension, Jesus told His disciples, "All authority has been given to Me in heaven and on earth" (Matthew 28:18). Then He commissioned them, and us, to make disciples of all nations. The authority of Jesus Christ abides today in His church. "He [God] put all things in subjection under His [Jesus'] feet, and gave Him as head over all things to the church, which is His body, the fullness of Him who fills all in all" (Ephesians 1:22–23).

When we understand the limitless spiritual authority we have in Christ, we will realize that none of the weapons of Satan formed against us can defeat us. If they do, it is because we let Satan win, not because he has more power than Christ. So no matter what you are facing right now, or what Satan is trying to do to you, you are not alone. Your High Priest in heaven is praying for you, asking the Father to give you all the strength you need. And you have access to the spiritual authority He died to secure for you to use.

This person of the cross—now resurrected and ascended to heaven, has received a crown as the King and is seated at the Father's right hand in the place of highest power and authority. This is the One through whom the prophets foretold and the types foreshadowed. This is the One through whom all things were made both in heaven and on earth, and all things have their being.

This is the uniquely divine yet undoubtedly human Christ of the cross.

PART 2

THE PURPOSE OF THE CROSS

5

THE ACCOMPLISHMENTS

VINCE LOMBARDI, THE legendary football coach of the Green Bay Packers, became very frustrated with his team's play one season and decided to address their performance. He did not think that they were living up to the level of their abilities. So one afternoon he called the men together in the locker room.

"It is obvious to me that we are missing something here. We need to get back to the basics." Then, holding up a football, he continued, "Gentlemen, this is a football."

Now that statement may seem elementary to professional football players who have been playing the game for years. But his point was that they were not performing at the level that they should. The Packers players were out on the field of play, but they had missed the basics—the fundamentals of the game.

As Christians, many of us are not living our lives at the level that God enables us to do. We are not expressing the fullness of the abundant life that Jesus Christ died to provide. One reason this is so is because while we have focused an inordinate amount of time and resources on creating a culture of Christianity, we have forgotten the basics. We have neglected the foundation.

When we fail to understand the core of our faith, and upon what that rests, we likewise fail to respond appropriately to life's scenarios.

I want you to envision in your mind's eye the cross of Jesus Christ as you hear these words: "Friends and fellow believers, this is the cross. It is the foundation upon which all else rests. It is the centerpiece of our faith and of all we are to think and do."

By "the cross" I am not merely referencing two pieces of wood. Neither am I referring to the icon atop a steeple that identifies a church, or the decoration hanging on your wall, or the jewelry around your neck.

> WE OFTEN FAIL TO FULLY APPLY THE CROSS'S PRACTICAL RELEVANCE FOR DAILY LIVING.

When I say "the cross," I am talking about the sacrificial atonement of Jesus Christ, and His subsequent resurrection.

The cross is the irreducible, substantive essence of our faith.

Sinners don't understand the cross because if they did, they would run to it. Many saints don't appreciate it because if they did, they would live differently in light of it They often fail to fully apply and appreciate its practical relevancy for daily living.

Why We Don't Value the Cross

At times we don't fully appreciate the cross because we don't fully recognize our need for it. And so we lower the value we ascribe to it. It's like breathing air. Every day you and I breathe in oxygen with relative ease. We don't have to create it. We don't have to buy it. We don't have to work for it. Nor do we have to go find it. It's right there for us to breathe every day. Our very lives depend on this substance, yet we spend little time thinking about it. Essentially, it's presumed upon.

That is unless you are like me and suffer at times from asthma. I've had asthma for as long as I can remember, and during those times of the worst asthma attacks, my attachment to oxygen becomes clear to me. In fact, oxygen is pretty much the only thing that I can think of during those moments. When breath no longer comes easy during an asthma attack, there is hardly a thing I wouldn't give in exchange for some oxyGenesis All of a sudden, the perceived value of oxygen has shot back up to where it more rightly belongs. After all, our lives are entirely dependent upon it.

The cross can be similar in many ways. It's a nice trinket or reminder during Communion that Jesus Christ loved us enough to die for us. It looks good on a wall or above a church. But we rarely talk about it, and I imagine that most of us rarely think about it as well. Its intrinsic value is absolute—without it we would all be dead in our trespasses and sins, yet its perceived value wanes as we shift in our mindset to a presumption of its presence. The reason why we can make this shift so easily is that we have forgotten our absolute need for the cross.

Before we look at what the cross of Christ accomplishes for us, we must understand our need for it based on (1) the holiness of God, (2) the law and our inability to keep it, and (3) the pervasiveness of our sin.

The Holiness of God

God's primary, core attribute—His controlling perfection—is His holiness. This is the only description of God found in the Scripture that is restated three times. God is never called "Love, Love, Love." Neither is He called "Peace, Peace, Peace." But He is called "Holy, Holy, Holy" in Isaiah 6:3. It is within this distinction that we discover the true necessity of the cross.

The word "holy" means to be in a class by itself. Holy speaks to the transcendent nature of God. It also speaks to His separateness from sin. Since God is holy by nature, righteousness is the revelation of both His nature and His standard.

This being so, God gave the law as a righteous standard to mankind. As we just read in Romans 3, His law manifests His holiness through revelation. Yet what humanity has sought to do over time is dumb down the law by lowering its standards. They somehow want to keep the blessings of God's name while ignoring the core of His nature. By reducing God's standard of holiness while simultaneously elevating mankind, they no longer have to deal with God *as* God.

Yet ultimately this works about as well as holding a beach ball under water. By trying to force a beach ball below water, you are actually ultimately propelling it farther out of the water when it comes back up. No matter how hard you try, a beach ball will never remain underwater on its own simply because of the laws of physics. Neither will God lower His own righteous standard due to His own holiness.

The Law

God's holy standard to which He holds us is written clearly in the book of Romans, where it says, "But now apart from the Law the righteousness of God has been *manifested*, being witnessed by the Law and the Prophets" (Romans 3:21, italics added) and, "For the wages of sin is death" (6:23). God has one standard: Perfection.

Keep in mind, the law was never given to us to make us righteous. On the contrary, the law reveals how unrighteous mankind really is. The law is like a mirror. A person goes to the mirror to see how messed up things are so that they can fix them. We see this truth revealed in Romans 3:20, "Because of the works of the Law no flesh will be justified in His sight; for through the Law comes the knowledge of sin."

The law was never designed to fix you. The law was designed to reveal what needed to be fixed. For example, when you drive down the road and pass a traffic sign that reads forty miles an hour, you won't find a policeman pulling you over to congratulate you for driving 40 mph or less. I've never had a cop pull me over just to say, "Tony, I want you to know that you are a spectacular citizen for driving at 40 mph or slower. Good job, Tony." Rather, if a policeman pulls anyone over, it is for breaking the law because the law (and the enforcers of the law) are not there to congratulate you, they are there to reveal when the standard has been broken.

Likewise, God's law isn't designed to make you righteous. What it is designed to do is to reveal your unrighteousness.

After all, it's easy these days to ignore unrighteousness. We do this in many ways, one of which is by not calling sin *sin*. We give it another name so it doesn't sound so bad anymore—like a mistake.

Yet beyond that, Scripture also tells us that even our so-called "righteous" actions are often polluted, either by a wrong motivation or intention. We read this in the book of Isaiah, "For all of us have become like one who is unclean, and all our righteous deeds are like a filthy garment" (64:6).

Our personal actions that are seen as "good" are regularly contaminated with attitudes and hearts that are not. We could be motivated by self-preservation, selfishness, or even pride. That's why Jesus revealed sin in a new light when He said, "You have heard that it was said, 'You shall not commit adultery'; but I say to you that everyone who looks at a woman with lust for her has already committed adultery with her in his heart'" (Matthew 5:27–28). Jesus took our understanding of sin to a new level through this and other statements. He let us know that God is not just looking at the external actions but that He is keenly in tune with our hearts and internal motivation.

87

Many believers may not have had a physical affair with someone, but I would imagine that there are many who have looked at another person with an attitude of lust, at some point in time. In God's viewpoint, our adulterous attitudes are in the same category as adultery itself.

> IN GOD'S VIEWPOINT, OUR ADULTEROUS ATTITUDES ARE IN THE SAME CATEGORY AS ADULTERY ITSELF.

Recognizing and accepting this truth would get many of us down off of our pedestals that allow us to so easily judge others, and more in line with God's viewpoint on ourselves. It would highlight our need for the cross and Christ's redemption in our lives. By aligning our perspective with God's perspective, we see more clearly what the cross of Jesus Christ accomplished for us.

The Scripture is blunt, "All have turned aside, together they have become useless; there is none who does good, there is not even one" (Romans 3:12; see Psalms 14:3; 53:2–3). There are no exceptions. We have all missed the mark. God measures each of us against His standard for righteousness, and in that case, none of us live up to it at all.

Whether it's original sin (Romans 5:14–18) or inherited sin birthed in our sin nature (Galatians 5:17; Psalm 51:5), we all sin. Whether it's sophisticated sin that dresses up in a suit or dress with the appearance of external spirituality while harboring jealousy, envy, and judgment in the heart, or whether it's sloppy sin displayed for all to see—it's all sin to God. He doesn't care if you look the part or not because God does not look at the outward appearance. God looks at the heart.

In fact, Jesus had some of His harshest words for those sinners who looked squeaky clean on the outside—in His day, the Pharisees. He told them, "You blind Pharisee, first clean the inside of the cup and of the dish, so that the outside of it may become clean also" (Matthew 23:26).

It's true that not everyone sins at the same level or to the same degree, yet how far will that get anyone if the standard is perfection? Let me illustrate it another way: If we were to all jump into the Pacific Ocean and tried to swim to Hawaii, would it matter that some of us got farther than the rest? No, it wouldn't matter at all. Because eventually we would all drown.

An Awareness of Sin

So why does God want us to have an awareness of sin? Why did He give us the law as a revealer not only of our actions but also of our hearts? Because it is in seeing our sin that we also see our need for our Savior.

For example, when you go to a jewelry store and ask to see a diamond, they will reach in the case, pull out the diamond, and almost always place it against a black cloth. There's a special reason why there is a dark cloth the jeweler uses in showing you the diamond. This is because the darker the backdrop, the more brilliant the diamond appears.

Similarly, God wants us to see clearly how sinful we are so that we can fully appreciate the significance of the cross. For whenever the awareness of our sinfulness is diminished, the cross gets lost. Its brilliance gets lost, and therefore, its effectiveness and power get lost. It also loses its power in our daily lives.

Through the atoning sacrifice of Jesus Christ, we are made pure. We read:

For while we were still helpless, at the right time Christ died for the ungodly. (Romans 5:6)

God demonstrates His own love toward us, in that while we were yet sinners, Christ died for us. (Romans 5:8)

For if while we were enemies we were reconciled to God through the death of His Son, much more, having been reconciled, we shall be saved by His life. (Romans 5:10)

He [Jesus] Himself is the propitiation for our sins; and not for ours only, but also for those of the whole world." (1 John 2:2)

who gave Himself for our sins so that He might rescue us from this present evil age, according to the will of our God and Father. (Galatians 1:4)

For Christ also died for sins once for all, the just for the unjust, so that He might bring us to God, having been put to death in the flesh, but made alive in the spirit. (1 Peter 3:18)

The cross refers to the atoning death of Christ for sin. But if you don't understand the standard of God and if you don't understand the sinfulness of man, you won't appreciate—nor will you benefit from—the death of Christ.

The First Accomplishment of the Cross: Justification

On the cross, Jesus Christ accomplished three specific things. Through His death, burial, and resurrection, He justified us, redeemed us, and propitiated us before God.

Justification is a legal concept involving the idea of justice. It also includes concepts of fairness and equity. The problem is that since the wages of sin is death, for us to be treated fairly and with equity as sinful beings before a holy God means that we deserve condemnation. Knowing this, God created an alternate path. He created a way to pacify, or satisfy, His wrath against us by carrying it out on a sinless sacrifice, Jesus Christ.

This path God created in order to legally acquit sinners of their sins is known as *imputation*, which means God attributed (or "credited") our sin onto Jesus Christ and attributed His righteousness onto us (2 Corinthians 5:21).

This can be understood by using an analogy from the financial sector as well. The Bible will often describe sin as a bill. For example, in the Lord's Prayer, we read, "Forgive us our debts." In Romans 6:23 we read that "the wages of sin is death."

You may have credit card debt that you owe to a bank, or debt on your car or home mortgage. Others may have paid off their mortgage. But we all have debt that we owe to God. This is because God's standard is nonnegotiable. He will not reduce His standard in order to make us feel better. Rather, out of His covenantal love (*hesed*). He covers our sin with His own alternative of justification through imputing righteousness through His Son. God "made Him who knew no sin to be sin on our behalf, so that we might become the righteousness of God in Him" (2 Corinthians 5:21).

Most of the time when we talk about the cross, we talk about Jesus bearing our sins, which He did (1 Peter 2:24). Yet He did more than that. In the verse we just looked at, Jesus "became" sin—or as it is literally translated, "He made Him who knew no sin *to be* sin." He was sin.

For thirty-three years, Jesus had lived in a sinful environment. He was exposed to sin on a daily basis yet He remained the perfect Son of God. In fact, He perfectly fulfilled the requirements of the law while on earth (Matthew 5:17; Romans 10:4). Yet on the cross, Jesus became sin.

The gravity of this reality is numbing when you bear in mind that there are roughly seven billion people currently on planet Earth. Likewise, the number of people who live on earth today is guessed to be equal to the amount of people who have lived on Earth since the beginning of time. Add those two figures and you have about fourteen billion people, all who have sinned numerous times and in numerous ways. That's not only a lot of people but that's a lot of sin.

All of the sins of fourteen billion people, on top of the sins of the people yet to be born—everything they have ever done and everything they wanted to do, and thought about doing—both motives and actions—were accumulated on that day when Jesus Christ hung on the cross. All of the sins of fourteen billion people, both actions and attitudes, were hurled at Christ on the cross. In addition to that, the sins of the people not yet born were collected and the sins that people have not yet committed were collected, to be imputed onto Jesus Christ so that we might be justified.

How bad was that moment? We often think that the pain of the cross was the cat-o'-nine-tails that lashed His back, or the thorns that ground into His skull, or the nails in His hands and feet. And all of that was excruciatingly painful, yes. But it was nothing compared to that one moment in time when Jesus looked up to heaven and cried out, "My God, My God, why have You forsaken me?" (Matthew 27:46).

At that moment, Jesus became sin. At that moment, the oneness of the Trinity was interrupted as Jesus looked up to the Father and asked why He had been abandoned. On the cross, when the whole world's sins were hurled at Jesus Christ, the Father turned His back on the Son and, in essence, told Jesus, "Go to hell." Because when Jesus died, that's exactly where He went.

That, my friend, is the pain of the cross. That is the sacrifice Jesus made on our behalf. And that is more than we could ever comprehend.

Jesus Christ experienced hell so that you and I could experience heaven.

Here, on this instrument of pain and shame, we behold the single greatest demonstration of sacrificial love ever made. Because of the cross, you and I now stand justified before God, as though we had never sinned. Even though we are sinners, when we trusted Christ for the forgiveness of sin and the free gift of eternal life, we have received a credit to cover our debts, and that credit is the righteousness of Christ.

> EVEN THOUGH WE ARE SINNERS, WE HAVE RECEIVED A CREDIT TO COVER OUR DEBTS, AND THAT CREDIT IS THE RIGHTEOUSNESS OF CHRIST.

Justification is the legal declaration that you are innocent even though you are guilty. This is because God came up with an alternate way to put the credit of righteousness onto your account, and He did this through the gift of grace. Paul wrote that we are "justified as a gift by His grace through the redemption which is in Christ Jesus" (Romans 3:24). Grace is the inexhaustible supply of God's goodness whereby He does for us what we cannot do for ourselves, making us just in His presence.

The Second Accomplishment: Redemption

Such justification comes about by Jesus' act of redemption on the cross. The word "redemption" in the Bible is generally used against a backdrop of slavery. In biblical days, slaves could often purchase their freedom. Either they could buy their own freedom, or someone else could purchase it for them, thus "redeeming" them. To redeem means to purchase through the payment of a price. The price of our salvation was the shed blood of Jesus Christ. On the cross, Jesus redeemed us from the slave market of sin.

The Greek word for redemption in Romans 3:24 is *apolytrosis*, which comes from two root words, *lytron* and *apo*. *Lytron* means a release through the payment of a price, or a ransom. The other root prefix, *apo*, refers to a separation. Adding *apo* means this is redemption at the most final level—a separation that destroys the union of two things and creates a great distance between the two.

Such a separation took place when the Jewish nation observed the Day of Atonement. The high priest would slay a goat and drain its blood, signifying the sacrifice for the sins of the nation of Israel. Afterward, the priest would put his hands on another goat, the scapegoat. We read in Leviticus that the priest would

> lay both of his hands on the head of the live goat, and confess over it all the iniquities of the sons of Israel and all their transgressions in regard to all their sins; and he [would] lay them on the head of the goat and send it away into the wilderness by the hand of a man who stands in readiness. The goat shall bear on itself all their iniquities to a solitary land; and he shall release the goat in the wilderness. (16:21–22)

The plan was straightforward enough: release the goat into the wilderness at a mountain called Azazel, which means "rugged" and "strong." In doing so, though, the chance existed that people might encounter the wandering goat at a later time, or the goat could even come back. Since the goat had a scarlet cloth tied to the top of its head, it could be easily identified. Historical recordings indicate that the Israelites dealt with this problem of scapegoats wandering back by taking the goat to Azazel and casting it down the side to its death thus creating a final *apo*, or separation.

Lytron secures our redemption from the sins committed before God. *Apo* means the penalty for those sins will not be coming back again because that penalty has been "separated" by a great distance. Together, *apolytrosis* is the complete, total, and final redemption secured on the cross by Jesus Christ. On the cross, He not only paid the penalty for our ransom from sin, but He removed that penalty for our sins as far away from us as the east is from the west (Psalm 103:12).

The Third Accomplishment: Propitiation

The third thing accomplished for us on the cross after justification and redemption is propitiation. We read this in Romans 3:25: "God displayed publicly [Christ Jesus] as a propitiation in His blood through faith." To understand propitiation, recall that God's justice has to be satisfied. His wrath automatically descends on unrighteousness simply because of His holy nature. Paul writes to the Romans, "For the wrath of God is revealed from heaven against all ungodliness and unrighteousness of men who suppress the truth in unrighteousness" (Romans 1:18).

How can God's wrath be satisfied? Through *propitiation*, a word that means "to satisfy, appease, or expiate." Christ's sacrifice is that propitiation.

A picture, or type (see page 50) of propitiation appears in the story of the Passover. The death angel visited Egypt to take the life of every firstborn child. But before this final plague upon the country, God told His people to slaughter a perfect lamb and to place its blood on the doorpost of their home. When they did that, the angel would then pass over that home and not claim the life of the firstborn within it. His judgment would skip that family because He was appeased with the blood of the lamb. This satisfied—provided propitiation—a holy God. But where there was no blood, there was no appeasement, and the full extent of God's wrath came upon that unprotected home.

Another illustration of this concept of propitiation occurred when Moses and his wife, Zipporah, were faced with the command to circumcise their son. Even though it was God asking him to do it, Moses would not circumcise his son and so God came after Moses with His wrath in order to judge him. Yet it says when Zipporah intervened and circumcised their son, God's wrath was then appeased and He turned aside (Exodus 4:24–26). His wrath was averted because someone had stepped in as a go-between to assuage it.

The story of Zipporah's propitiation shows us two truths: (1) God's wrath can be averted, and (2) someone else can step in and act on behalf of another. That is exactly what Jesus Christ did for us on the cross. He turned the wrath of God from us and onto Himself in order to be the propitiation for our sins as well as the sins of the whole world (1 John 2:2).

When Jesus Christ died on the cross, He received the judgment that was due us. The flames of God's wrath will not reach those who take their stand on the cross of Christ. He has removed the penalty for our sins and satisfied God's wrath toward sin. Because of Jesus' propitiation, we not only have nothing to fear with regard to eternity, but we have been given so great a salvation to live out on earth.

6

THE IDENTIFICATION

A MAN SCHEDULED AN appointment to see a psychiatrist, telling the receptionist he was having "serious problems." When he finally took a seat in the psychiatrist's cozy and neatly decorated office days later, he looked cautiously at the doctor.

"Doc," he said. The doctor kept his eyes on his patient and nodded his head, urging him gently to continue.

"Doc, something's wrong," the man blurted out.

"What's the problem, sir?" the doctor asked, trying to get more information.

"Well, every time I go to the supermarket, I am drawn to the dog food. I just want to be around the dog food. In fact, I love to eat dog food."

The doctor shifted his weight in his chair and decided to search for some background on this man's issue. "How long have you been struggling with this problem?" the doctor asked patiently.

"Ever since I was a puppy," the man replied.

You see, how you perceive yourself will determine what you seek after. If you perceive yourself as a puppy, then you will naturally want to find some dog food. In other words, your identity is critical to your behavior, habits, and ways of operating.

Many Christians today are confused about who they are, which in turn brings about confusion in how they are to function. We function the way we do because of how we perceive ourselves. This means that if our self-perception is incorrect, our function will be errant as well.

We often want to change what we do without having a clear understanding of who we are. This is actually operating in reverse. When a Christian says, "I am an addict," then we should not be surprised that he or she acts that addiction out because that is who we were told that they were. Your self-identification influences your practice. What you think influences what you do.

In fact, a friend of mine works at a drug rehab center—one of the best in the nation—that uses nothing more than Scripture to help their patients overcome their addictions. This is because when you meditate on and memorize the truth of who you are and the power of the One who loves you, you have all you need to live a victorious life. The mind is a powerful thing. It is the root of all defeats as well as all successes.

Therefore, to achieve the greatness that God has in store for you, rather than settle for just getting by, you must first change what you think. In particular, you must change what you think about the cross of Christ. As we looked at in the previous chapter, the cross of Jesus Christ is just as relevant today as it was two thousand years ago. It is not simply an icon around which we celebrate Easter each year. Rather, it is the very definition of your success as a believer. It is to be the centerpiece of your personal reference and your identity.

The summing up of who you are as a Christian and who God has designed you to be is found in Galatians 2:20. This is my life verse. In fact, before my feet hit the floor each morning, I regularly say this verse as a reminder of who I am and how I am to approach my day. Before we look at this verse, though, let's consider its context. Beginning in verse 11 of Galatians 2, we discover the disciple Peter had been eating ham sandwiches, chittlins, and pigs' feet with the Gentiles. Peter was enjoying a good meal of food he did not typically eat (pork) with a group of people whom Jews did not typically associate with. He did so to be gracious and because God had in a dream revealed that pork was no longer unclean (see Acts 10:10–16, 24–29). While eating, some of his Jewish brothers show up, and not wanting to offend his own race, Peter withdraws from his association with the Gentiles. In essence, he caves to peer pressure.

Seeing what he did, Paul confronts Peter. We read that Peter "stood condemned" (Galatians 2:11). It wasn't that Peter wasn't a Christian or that he wasn't saved; the issue was that Peter was not functioning in light of his identification with his faith. Rather, he was functioning in light of his identification with his culture. We know this because Paul went on to write, "But when I saw that they were not straightforward about the truth of the gospel" (Galatians 2:14).

In other words, when Paul saw that Peter and his friends' social decision (who they were going to eat with) wasn't being defined by their gospel belief system, they were then warping the message and testimony of what the gospel means in everyday life. There was a spiritual, theological issue that brought rise to a social problem. All social, economic, familial, political, personal, and other issues can be traced back to a spiritual and theological root. One of our problems today is our unwillingness, or possibly our ignorance, in properly connecting the social and the spiritual. We must reach out without compromising our faith. We must fully identify with the cross or we remove the power that comes through our alignment with Jesus Christ.

Crucifixion and Identification

If you received Jesus Christ as your Savior, a crucifixion has occurred. In fact, two crucifixions have occurred—Jesus on the cross, and you. Paul tells Peter and us in Galatians 2:20 what the secret to living a life of power and purpose really is when he writes, "I have been crucified with Christ; and it is no longer I who live, but Christ lives in me; and the life which I now live in the flesh I live by faith in the Son of God, who loved me and gave Himself up for me."

Through the cross, a dual death has occurred. In the spiritual realm, what happened in history some two thousand years ago has happened in you the moment you trusted Jesus Christ for your salvation. A union has occurred that is both theological and practical. In fact, it may be the most important practical application of Scripture that you could ever know. The key to all things related to life, victory, and power lie in this one truth revealed in Galatians 2:20.

When you accepted Jesus Christ as your Savior, a legal transaction occurred. You were justified because of His blood sacrifice and made one with Him. This is similar to a marriage when two people are united and become "one flesh" as demonstrated in physical intimacy. The problems in marriage typically arise when one or both parties try to live other than as "one flesh."

The problems in your Christian life result from the same issue; however, since Jesus Christ is the perfect, sinless Deity—a separation happens solely when you try to live apart from Him.

Once you've stepped into the family of God, you are a new creation made one with Christ. Yet you have brought a lot of your self-centered thinking, actions, fears, anxieties, and desires into the new relationship. Similar to a daughter who marries young, you are inclined to falling back on the history of what you've known and experienced before your union with Christ. A daughter who spent twenty-some years in the influence and care of her father may struggle to transfer that allegiance and identity to her young husband. This, as you may know or have seen, causes great conflict in a marriage. Likewise, a similar mentality of bringing your way of thinking, acting, and believing into your relationship with

Jesus Christ sets up a series of conflicts as well.

To be crucified with Jesus Christ establishes a brand-new reference point for how you view yourself, others, your circumstances, and life. When I drink coffee in the morning, I will always locate some cream or some milk to pour into my coffee. After I stir it, my coffee and the cream are now one. There is no way that I could possibly disconnect my coffee from my cream once I've stirred it. However, what many believers will do in their Christian lives is become one with Jesus Christ at salvation and then attempt to disconnect Him from their thinking, actions, choices, decisions, and all else in their lives. The union is still there, of course. But they wind up with a big mess and a lot of wasted time and effort.

Dying Daily to Ourselves

Paul the apostle gives us the secret to the success of maximizing our union with the cross in 1 Corinthians when he says, "I die daily" (1 Corinthians 15:31). To be crucified means to die, and according to Paul that death ought to be daily. To die simply means to abandon our wants, thoughts, and motives, and pick up His wants, thoughts, and motives instead. In dying to self, you and I are able to truly live. Jesus' life in us comes only when we willingly lay down our own life and submit to Him, when we choose His will over our own. It is a conscious decision to let God's way supersede our way, to let God's choice supersede our choice. In such surrender we will experience the abundant life (John 10:10) that has been promised to us through the death and resurrection of Jesus Christ.

So many of us fail to carry this out and then wonder why we are not experiencing all of God's promises. We die to Him in salvation but then we live for ourselves in our daily choices. We wonder why we fail to have the victory that is ours and live instead in perpetual defeat. It is because there can be no resurrection without a crucifixion. You don't get the miracle without the surrender.

You probably own different appliances. Each appliance has a unique responsibility. The refrigerator keeps things cold. The stove makes things hot. The toaster toasts things. Can openers open things, and so on. But there is one thing that each appliance holds in common—none of them functions for itself. Each appliance that you have purchased exists to serve you. If it didn't, my guess is that you would no longer have it in your home.

The reason you bought those appliances was to benefit from them. The purpose for the purchase was to benefit the purchaser.

> AS LONG AS YOU ARE LIVING FOR YOU, ALL THAT THE CROSS HAS TO OFFER WILL NEVER BE YOURS.

Friend, you were bought with a price (see 1 Corinthians 6:20), the shed blood of Jesus Christ. You exist for the Purchaser, not for yourself. The moment you flip that and begin thinking *I exist for myself*, you have lost your identity. You have lost the reason for you being here. You will never experience all that the Christian life was meant to be. You will never realize all of the power that you are supposed to have until you realize that you do not exist for you. As long as you are living for you, all that the cross has to offer will never be yours. It will remain as a historical event that happened some two thousand years ago rather than as a daily experience ushering you into the greatest moments and meaning of your life.

If you were to ask Paul what his plans were for the day, he would reply, "I don't have plans, because dead people don't plan." Yet if you changed the question a little bit and said, "Paul, what are God's plans for you?" he would say, "Okay, let's talk." Paul aligned his thinking with God's thinking. He made God's will his will. He made seeking God's face and God's perspective as the single most important thing in his life.

Paul got it. He understood what it meant to identify with the cross of Christ, and because he did, he received all that was his to receive in Christ Jesus.

A Back, a Bar, and a Pole

A key to understanding how to identify with the cross comes when Paul continues on in Galatians 2:20 and says, "The life which I now live in the flesh I live by faith in the Son of God, who loved me and gave Himself up for me." The King James Version translates the verse, "I live by the faith of the Son of God." The word "of" is a more accurate translation of the original text and gives a clearer definition of how we are to live our lives victoriously. What Paul means when he says that he lives by faith "of" the Son of God is that he lives each day not so much by his own faith in Jesus but by his faith in Jesus' faith in Jesus.

I know that may sound a little tricky but the truth it contains is profound. It is not just that we are to believe in Jesus Christ, but we are to believe in Jesus' belief in Himself. It is because of your full confidence that Jesus has full confidence in Himself that you discover the ability to piggyback on Him.

Have you ever taken a child on a piggyback ride? Do you know what that child believes in? That child is not just believing in you, he or she is believing that you believe in you. They believe that you have confidence in you. That is why they will ask, "Do you have me?" In other words, your little girl, your little guy is asking, "Do you believe that you have me?" This is because even though they may have doubts, if you believe, then they will believe in your belief.

It's not simply your faith in Jesus that gives you the ability to experience the abundant life. It is your faith in Jesus' faith in Himself that opens that door. You don't have to worry about how much faith you have—even weak faith can accomplish much if it is placed on that which is worthy of it. Jesus said that faith as small as a mustard seed can move a mountain. It's not the size of your faith that matters, it is the object of your faith that matters. That is the key. If you have a lot of faith in a little thing, you don't have enough to do anything. But if you have a little faith in a big thing, then you have more than enough to do everything.

Even if your faith in Jesus is small, it will still work wonders because Jesus' faith in Jesus is huge. Don't worry about how much faith you have, worry about what you place it in. Piggyback on Jesus because He's got you.

For example, a high jumper typically tries to clear seven feet. He backs up, gets in his stance, takes off running, lifts his foot up, and then jumps with all of the effort that he can muster in order to leap as high as he can. The high jumper believes he can do it and he does as much as he can. If he knocks over the bar, he goes back and tries harder the next time.

Yet, when a pole-vaulter tries to clear a bar, he will try to get over a much higher level, even more than double of what the high jumper will attempt. This is because the pole-vaulter has a pole in his hands and he is not merely resting on his own ability to make it. He is resting in his confidence in the pole, that it has enough strength and elasticity to do what is needed to propel him to victory. The pole-vaulter is relying on what he has his hands on rather than simply on himself. Because of this, he is able to go higher and farther than he ever could on his own.

Too many Christians today are trying to get by on their own. Maybe you are one of them. You run as fast as you can, jump as high as you can, and work as hard as you can but don't go nearly as far as you can were you to rely on your attachment to the cross of Jesus Christ. If you will link yourself up with the pole of His cross, He has the ability and the willingness to propel you higher than you ever thought you could soar. But that takes faith. It takes dependence. It takes identifying with Him daily over identifying with yourself, the world, your friends, or anything else that you place before Him.

When you do, though, you will not regret it. It is because of his intimate and daily identification with Jesus Christ and the meaning behind His cross that Paul was able to write in his letter to the church at Philippi, "I can do all things through Him who strengthens me" (Philippians 4:13).

For most Christians, that is just a cute saying. It is a nice sounding spiritual platitude to quote. I have met precious few believers who take it literally and comprehend how to live the full life of identification with Jesus Christ so that they experience the fullness of His power.

But for Paul, that was not just a cute thing to say. Paul knew that he had an attachment to a pole that could hurl him higher than he could ever get on his own. In fact, it hurled him so high that he wound up in the third heaven (see 2 Corinthians 12:1–2). This happened not because Paul had a whole bunch of faith but rather because Paul believed that Jesus had faith in Himself. Paul tells us that it is Christ in him, and Christ in you, that produces the faith for victory.

How to Function Supernaturally: Christ in You

In his letter to the church at Colossae, he writes, "To whom God willed to make known what is the riches of the glory of this mystery among the Gentiles, which is Christ in you, the hope of glory" (Colossians 1:27). Paul's goal for the believers he was ministering to and encouraging was that Christ would be manifest in their mortal bodies. This is because when Jesus Christ is made manifest in a believer's life, the believer begins to function supernaturally rather than naturally. They have access to the abundant life promised in Scripture through abiding with Christ.

What keeps Jesus Christ from being made manifest in your life? It is when you do not die daily to yourself. When you do not become crucified with Him on an ongoing basis. That is the greatest deterrent to experiencing all of the supernatural power and victory God has in store for you.

As long as you are living for yourself and the cross remains a distant thought from an even more distant past, you will not fully maximize the life you were made to live.

Friend, you can't identify with the cross of Jesus by rules. In fact, the cross ended the system of rules and replaced it with a relationship. You can't achieve this victory or access this power through checking off a list of rules. It happens only through love that both honors and trusts in Jesus' belief in Himself and what He has done.

Some say that the cross alone is not enough. But that diminishes what the cross attained. To add anything to the cross—to add works, self-righteousness, duty—is to nullify the fullness of His love for you. It is to spit on the cross. I know that is a graphic way to look at what you think you might be doing to live a Christian life, but the cross accomplished everything for you already. To add to it is to lessen what Jesus already did. Paul followed up after his verse on being crucified with Christ with this very thought "I do not nullify the grace of God, for if righteousness comes through the Law, then Christ died needlessly" (Galatians 2:21). To nullify something is to cancel it out. When you pursue religion over a relationship with Jesus Christ, you have canceled out the grace of God in your life that the cross of Christ achieved for you.

God is free to rain down His grace upon you because of what Jesus did on the cross. You have hope simply because Christ is in you—"Christ in you, the hope of glory" (Colossians 1:27). In order for God's power and grace to flow, your focus must be on Him. It must be on Jesus. It must be on the cross. Your identity must daily be in His crucifixion.

> THE BAD NEWS IN CHRISTIANITY TODAY IS THAT FEW CHRISTIANS SEEM TO INTIMATELY KNOW JESUS.

The bad news in Christianity today from what I can tell is that few Christians seem to intimately know Jesus. Jesus is not in the vicinity simply because there is no living connection to Him. Yes, there is a legal tie, but there is no love relationship. When you cancel the relationship, you cancel—or nullify—the flow of God's power to you.

Connected to the Power

Let me explain this with a concrete example. Let's say your refrigerator is not working. Your ice cream is melting, and your food is beginning to spoil. So you go online and you research how to fix your refrigerator. You find a manual for your model and it shows you all of the parts of your refrigerator. You spend a lot of time studying this manual. You read the book thoroughly, and as you do you attempt to apply what you learned. You twist that or turn this; you move that and adjust this. Yet no matter how much you apply from this book, nothing seems to be working. And your food rots even further.

Then someone comes up to you and gives you a suggestion. "Why don't you plug it in?"

Friend, no matter how hard you try, you will have only wasted your time and your life if you do not live connected to the power of the cross in Jesus Christ. You can come to church every day of the week if you want to. You can read the Bible from cover to cover. You can study it, repeat it, and tell others about it. In fact, you can try to do what it says to do all day long. But if you have canceled the flow of God's grace in your life due to a nullification of the cross and your relationship with Jesus Christ, it won't mean a thing.

God is not free to flow His power through you if you are not identified with the cross. Until you make the decision that you will die to yourself and live to Him, you will continue to simply exist rather than maximize God's good plans for you.

A lot of believers today are blocking what God wants to do in them and through them because they are trying to get there in their own strength. In doing so they cut the cord through which grace flows. Doing the best you can and trying harder every day is not what God wants from you. He wants your heart. He wants your surrender to Him. He wants you to trust Him, love Him, and experience Him. He wants a relationship, and in that relationship you will have all that is yours—all by virtue of Christ's sacrifice on the cross.

7

THE AUTHORITY

MY CALLING, SINCE I was eighteen years old, has always been to preach. Whether that means delivering God's Word at our church on Sundays or Wednesdays, or traveling to preach in venues and churches on the road—you can find me preaching several times each week.

With those travels, as you might imagine, I have become intimately acquainted with American Airlines. That's why I wasn't surprised some time ago when I received a packet from the airline in the mail. This particular packet focused on the advantages that come to me as a "platinum" frequent flyer. It was a book of benefits that had accrued to me due to the large number of miles I had flown.

At first, I just tossed the booklet to the side on a stack of papers. It didn't pique my interest at the start. All that concerned me was knowing how to get on the plane and get to my destination. I figured what I knew in my head about flying American was as good as what was in the packet.

A few weeks later, I came across the packet again. For some reason, this time I decided to start thumbing through it. Soon I discovered that there are a number of benefits that I was not aware of. In fact, significant opportunities existed for "going platinum" that I was not using. The airline was offering me upgrade options, booking options, and priority

THE POWER OF THE CROSS

access options, among other things. These benefits had been there for me to utilize all along. I had just never used them because I had failed to investigate what my relationship offered.

Without fully knowing the privileges of my platinum-level relationship with American Airlines, I had failed to completely experience and maximize my inheritance from the airline.

Similarly many Christians come to church every week, unaware of all the rights and privileges that the cross affords them. They fail to utilize the benefits that God has ordained and bequeathed to His saints. Knowing about the cross without knowing the authority and benefits of the cross will keep you from experiencing all that God has in store for you.

The cross provides to you and me the opportunity to see what God can do beyond the normal, everyday routine of life. The cross is the key to God invading the difficult or mundane circumstances of life just like He invaded the tomb of Jesus when He died on the cross, flipping things around in order to reveal His power and authority.

> THE CROSS IS THE KEY TO GOD INVADING THE DIFFICULT OR MUNDANE CIRCUMSTANCES OF LIFE.

A lot of Christians sing about God's power and talk about God's power, but can never testify to experiencing God's power because they have never accessed God's power. They have never seen Him turn, twist, or tweak things beyond their human comprehension.

Have you ever watched an action-adventure film where the hero of the story is trying to locate a special artifact or treasure? All along the way, he or she faces much opposition from the enemy, who is trying to divert our hero from reaching the goal and receiving the prize.

These films often remind me of what Satan attempts to do in the lives of believers. You and I truly have a precious treasure—a unique possession—that our enemy doesn't want us to discover. We have things available to us that he doesn't want us to get. He will use every means to stop us from picking up the treasure that God has for us.

The Treasure of the Cross

Paul gives us some insight into the benefits and authority that the treasure of the cross has to offer in his letter to the church at Ephesus. Now the opening of this letter may not have received a passing grade in an English course. In Ephesians 1:3–14, Paul writes one very long run-on sentence in the original Greek language. It could be that he was so impassioned about what he was saying that he didn't even take the time to pause between words. He goes on and on. He just can't seem to quit.

It makes sense for Paul to be beside himself concerning this topic, though, because what Paul shares is worthy of excitement. He tells us of the authority, benefits, and prized possessions that we have because of the cross.

Here is the full sentence, now with sentence breaks inserted into the English translation:

Blessed be the God and Father of our Lord Jesus Christ, who has blessed us with every spiritual blessing in the heavenly places in Christ, just as He chose us in Him before the foundation of the world, that we would be holy and blameless before Him. In love He predestined us to adoption as sons through Jesus Christ to Himself, according to the kind intention of His will, to the praise of the glory of His grace, which He freely bestowed on us in the Beloved. In Him we have redemption through His blood, the forgiveness of our trespasses, according to the riches of His grace which He lavished on us. In all wisdom and insight He made known to us the mystery of His will, according to His kind intention which He purposed in Him with a view to an administration suitable to the fullness of the times, that is, the summing up of all things in Christ, things in the heavens and things on the earth. In Him also we have obtained an inheritance, having been predestined according to His purpose who works all things after the counsel of His will, to the end that we who were the first to hope in Christ would be to the praise of His glory. In Him, you also, after listening to the message of truth, the gospel of your salvation—having also believed, you were sealed in Him with the Holy Spirit of promise, who is given as a pledge of our inheritance, with a view to the redemption of God's own possession, to the praise of His glory.

After Paul reaches the end of his long, run-on sentence, he gives thanks for their faith and love for each other, as well as noting how he mentions them in his prayers (vv. 15–17). Then he makes a pointed statement. He asks that God will open "the eyes of [the] hearts" of those to whom he is addressing his letter so that they will know what all they have gained through Christ's atonement on the cross: "that you will know what is the hope of His calling, what are the riches of the glory of His inheritance in the saints, and what is the surpassing greatness of His power toward us who believe" (vv. 18–19).

Similar to me not knowing what benefits I had accrued as an American Airlines platinum flyer and thus not being able to access those benefits, Paul did not want believers to go without access to the strength, power, and greatness God has in store for us.

In other words, Paul was saying that God doesn't want you to have to go to heaven before you get to taste it on earth. He has laid up for you a "pledge of [your] inheritance" (v. 14) to access right now. In Greek, the word "pledge" can mean a "down payment." Through the cross, God has set aside a "down payment" on heaven for you to receive while on earth. As a believer, you are on your way to heaven. However, God does not want you to have to wait to get there in order to feel and experience what heaven is like. There is a piece of heaven that has been allocated to you right now.

"The Surpassing Greatness"

Are you curious what that down payment is? Or what has already been put in the will for you as a pledge of your inheritance? Paul summed it up at the end of his treatise on salvation when he said it involved, "the hope of His calling, what are the riches of the glory of His inheritance in the saints, and what is the surpassing greatness of His power" (vv. 18–19).

Notice that he didn't write that God wanted us to experience His power. Rather, he wrote that God wants us to experience the "surpassing greatness" of His power. He wants us to know that when it comes to God, He can bring things out of nowhere to turn things around in each of our lives. He is the only true Super Power. No believer should ever settle for being an average individual. God has destined you for greatness through the "surpassing greatness" of His power.

The "surpassing greatness to us who believe" began after Calvary. Jesus was crucified and nailed to a cross on Friday. Friday was a bad day. Friday was a shameful day. Friday was a lonely day. Friday looked like it was the last day. It was a bad day physically—Jesus was beaten to a pulp. It was a bad day emotionally—Scripture says Christ cried tears of blood. It was a bad day spiritually—He was separated from God, the Father.

However, Friday did not determine where Jesus would wind up.

This is because Paul went on to describe just what the "surpassing greatness" of God's power looks like when he summarized it in what happened to Jesus on the cross. He wrote,

These [the surpassing greatness of His power] are in accordance with the working of the strength of His might which He brought about in Christ, when He raised Him from the dead and seated Him at His right hand in the heavenly places, far above all rule and authority and power and dominion, and every name that is named, not only in this age but also in the one to come." (Ephesians 1:19–21)

Essentially, what started off bad on Friday wound up being awesome on Sunday. This is because God reversed the effects of Friday, raising Christ from the dead and seating Him in the heavenlies.

Some of you reading these few pages may feel beaten down or broken. Some of you may have experienced an emotional beating, a physical beating, a relational beating, or even a spiritual beating. You feel broken down; the circumstances of your life have not been in your favor.

But what I want you to know is what the apostle Paul wants you to know: the surpassing greatness of God's power that raised Christ from the dead, turning death into life is also available to you. God flipped the script with Jesus, and He can do the same with you.

Are you experiencing a death in your life? Or what feels like a crucifixion? Have you had a death in your dreams, relationships, home, career, finances, health, or in any other way? The message of the cross is that God has enough power to turn even the worst scenario into a victory if you will but trust Him.

The Doctrine of the Ascension

With the cross, we have the doctrine of the death—but it is followed by the doctrine of the resurrection. Yet what we often fail to appeal to and benefit from fully is the doctrine of the ascension (discussed in detail in chapter 5). Jesus didn't just rise from the dead. Rather, He rose and then was taken up into heaven and seated at the right hand of the Father.

While that may not sound like a lot, it is. In the Old Testament days, when the priest went into the presence of God, you would find a lot of furniture inside the temple, but what you wouldn't find was a chair. The priest couldn't sit down because his work was never finished. Therefore, there was no provision for him to sit down. However, when Jesus entered heaven, He was told to take up a seat and settle in. Christ's work on earth was finished. As He said on the cross, "It is finished!" (John 19:30; Gk. *tetelesti*).

But what does Jesus' dying on the cross, being raised, and then sitting down in heaven have to do with you? Everything. See, the Bible's Old Testament presents the old covenant. Here, everyone was looking futuristically toward God's final provision. All of the sacrifices, ceremonies, rituals, and actions were done in anticipation of God's tangible entrance into history.

In the New Testament the new covenant appears. It is all tied to your relationship to the cross. When you lose sight of what happened there, you can't fully experience it here. You lose sight of what Jesus accomplished on the cross, and you will lose sight of your inheritance, available right now.

His Authority above All Others

Friend, whatever it is that you are dealing with, or whomever it is that you are dealing with, that person or situation does not have the last say. No matter how big, powerful, or pushy they are or the situation seems to be, Jesus Christ is sitting far above all of it. He is positioned higher than all rule, authority, dominion, and power. He has the authority.

For example, the president of the United States sits in the Oval Office at the White House yet what he decrees from there—an investigation or a declaration—can impact you wherever you live. It may even impact people halfway around the world. This is because the president sits in a powerful location, above all other authorities in our nation. If one man in one city can affect an entire nation, or even the world, politically, what do you think that the King of kings and the Lord of lords can do sitting far above all rule and authority?

That means that whatever your enemy, opposition, circumstance, or challenge has to say is *a* word, it is just not *the final* word. Your boss may have a word, but he doesn't have the final word. Your doctor may have a word, but he doesn't have the final word. Your finances may have a word, but they don't have the final word. Your emotions may have *a* word, but they don't have the final word.

What the cross accomplished for you and for me is authority. Keep in mind, authority has to do with power, but authority does not simply mean power. Authority is the right to use the power that you possess. For example, referees are not the strongest men on the football field. In fact, they are older, slower, and heavier. Yet when a referee throws out a yellow flag on a player who is much bigger than he, the bigger player has to yield. The faster player has to slow down. This is because the referee has a greater power called authority. Authority overrules power.

Jesus' Authority over Satan

Now the devil is bigger than you. He is more powerful than you. He is more cunning than you. He is stronger than you. You can't overrule the devil with your power, and I would caution you not to try. However, when you are identified with Christ—His cross, resurrection, and ascension—you are now identified with the authority that overrides Satan's power.

What Satan tries to do, however, is to get you thinking that the cross is something that belongs in the annals of history rather than in the events of today. Satan doesn't mind if you pay homage to the cross, he just doesn't want you to access the benefits and inheritance that are due you through it. That way he can continue to intimidate you with his power without you realizing that Christ's authority trumps him.

What Satan does is similar to a man holding a gun on you. At first, you may feel afraid and at this man's mercy. Yet if someone were to point out to you that the man's gun did not have any bullets in it, he would no longer control you. Similarly, at the cross, Jesus Christ "disarmed" Satan (Colossians 2:15). Jesus Christ removed the bullets from Satan's gun. Satan still likes to play like a tough guy and try to intimidate everyone with his power, but ultimately, Jesus Christ has stripped him of his authority. Therefore, his power is only as strong as he can persuade you to believe that it is. In itself, his power is not strong enough to overcome Christ's authority.

When Satan comes at you, remember that he is coming with an unloaded gun. Of course, he's not going to tell you that. He wants you to think that you're never going to overcome, or that you will always be defeated. He wants you to think that since depression is in your family history, that you will always fall victim to it, or to overspending, overeating, or financial devastation.

But what Jesus wants you to know is that there are no bullets in that gun! Satan was disarmed at Calvary. Satan no longer has the last word because Jesus Christ now sits high above all rule and authority. And you and I are seated with Him sharing in that authority.

Am I saying that you will have no problems? No. What I am saying is that if you will fix your eyes on Jesus, even though you have problems, He will place you above your circumstances rather than under them.

One way to bring this victory about even faster is to praise God. Not for the bad day, circumstance, or problem. But praise Him because it is not the last word. Praise Him because He is seated high above all rule and authority, and by virtue of your relationship with Him, you are seated with Him and therefore have access to His rule and authority in your life (Ephesians 2:6). This is why we read in Revelation that the believers were able to overcome Satan:

> Now the salvation, and the power, and the kingdom of our God and the authority of His Christ have come, for the accuser of our brethren has been thrown down, he who accuses them before our God day and night. And *they overcame him because of the blood of the Lamb*. (Revelation 12:10–11, italics added)

When the passage states that they overcame him "because of the blood of the Lamb," it is referencing the cross. They overcame Satan because they never lost sight that the very thing that was set out to bring hell into their lives did not have the last word. They never lost sight that the cross has conquered Satan, granting them access to an authority higher than his own.

Our Authority through Him

What God wants us to know through these passages in Colossians, Ephesians, and Revelation is that the cross of Jesus Christ has provided victory for you over your enemies, including Satan. Because Jesus Christ is seated above all rule and authority, we too are seated there with Him. In fact, Paul states exactly that as he continues his letter to the church at Ephesus. He writes in chapter 2, "Even when we were dead in our transgressions, made us alive together with Christ (by grace you have been saved), and raised us up with Him, and seated us with Him in the heavenly places in Christ Jesus, so that in the ages to come He might show the surpassing riches of His grace in kindness toward us in Christ Jesus" (vv. 5–7).

Not only does Jesus Christ have a chair in heaven to sit down in but you have a chair there as well. You have been "seated . . . with Him" above all rule and authority. You have been spiritually relocated. You might be saying, "If I'm seated up there with Jesus, Tony, then why am I not experiencing the victory?" The answer is simple—the same reason why I did not experience the benefits and privileges afforded to me as an American Airlines platinum flyer until I learned what those benefits were and accessed them. If you don't know where you are seated and what exactly that means, you won't access the authority that is yours for the asking.

Physically, you are on earth. Yet spiritually you are in heavenly places. This is like the common communication portal of teleconferencing. Over the years, teleconferencing has become highly sophisticated, but even in its infancy it provided us with the ability to transcend space and location like never before. I could be sitting in my office in Dallas and yet be entirely and coherently present in a board meeting for an organization in Chicago through this means. This is because the method provided the opportunity to be in dual locations at one time.

Likewise, you and I are physically positioned on earth yet we are also in heavenly places. However, unless you realize that and operate out of that mindset, you will be confined to what earth has to offer. You must approach your life spiritually in order to attain spiritual authority. If all you see is what you see then you will never see all there is to be seen. If your eyes are focused on the here and now, you will miss experiencing heaven's rule in history. Earth's seat doesn't give you authority. Only heaven has access to that authority because of what Jesus accomplished on the cross.

When you learn how to function in connection with divine authority, it changes everything. It changes the intimidation factor that others may have over you. It changes your fear and worry levels. In fact, when I know deep in my spirit that God has shown me something that He is going to do or arrange, the fact that other people say it isn't going to happen or that it can't happen doesn't bother me. What other people have to say becomes irrelevant when you function according to the authority of the cross.

When you live in light of Christ's authority, gained for you at the cross, it will change how you walk, talk, and think. It will change your whole approach to life because you realize the difference between power and authority. You realize that what appears to have control in your life doesn't have the ultimate control. What appears to have a say in your finances, emotions, health, home, or elsewhere doesn't have the last say.

Friend, before you give up, look up. Fix your eyes on Jesus and see yourself seated with Him in the heavenlies, granted full access to His rule and authority according to the power of God that works in you.

8

THE RELEASE

ONE DAY A MAN arrived in America for a vacation tour. In the country where he had grown up, the military enforced a curfew; after a certain time each night, they cleared the streets and everyone stayed in their homes.

Yet when this man visited the United States, he brought the old law with him. He failed to realize a curfew was no longer in place. Each day Frederick would visit different places in this new land only to rush back to his hotel each night before dark.

One day he stayed out longer than he thought he should. When he realized the lateness of the hour, Frederick sought to catch a cab back as fast as he could. Once inside the taxi, he told the driver, "Please get me back to the hotel before the curfew." The driver couldn't figure out what he was talking about. So he asked Frederick to describe the curfew to him. When Frederick did, the driver realized that this visitor had brought the law of his homeland into the new one. He was mixing his old life with the new.

That's when the cab driver took the time to tell Frederick that in the United States, the law that he had been raised with and was used to no longer applied. He was no longer under the jurisdiction of his homeland. He was in a new land now, and that meant that he was free to stay up and stay out as late as he wanted to. The restrictions of his country no longer applied.

The reason why this man was still bound in the midst of freedom was because he had not yet learned to cast off the chains of the old.

Unfortunately, this is a similar reality for many of us Christians. Even though we have a new life of freedom through Christ, we have not yet learned how to release the bondage of being in Adam. So while there may be talk about freedom and even strong desires for freedom, the overarching pressure of the curfew of bondage underneath the law remains firm.

Far too many believers today are in hostage to the manacles of legalism simply because they have spent so much time in the old country that they have failed to realize the freedom the cross of Jesus Christ now provides.

Escaping Legalism through the Cross

When a person truly learns how to live in light of the cross and enters into what many call the "exchanged life," they shift from an old regime into a new freedom. They shift from the concept, confusion, and consequences of legalism into a life of grace.

If you are a legalist, you will never know freedom. If legalism—acting according to rules in an attempt to please God and others—is your modus operandi, then the Christian life will be a burden on your back. (For a fuller definition and discussion of legalism, see the section "Legalism Defined.") You will never discover the joy of a life full of grace. Grace is a gift far too many people do not open and enjoy. For some, it is too good to be true. For others, it is too broad to be understood. And for still others, grace is simply too much of a gift to feel they have a right to receive it.

No other person this side of heaven lived out the fullness of grace than the apostle Paul. His life and ministry demonstrate the full power of grace like none other, so we turn to him to learn about this ever important topic, focusing on his letter to the church at Galatia (Galatians 1:2).

He begins with a focus on the good news of the death and resurrection of Jesus Christ. Despite the supreme gift of Christ's sacrifice, the people who comprise the church in Galatia have turned toward another belief system, similar to that of the Judaizers. The Judaizers and Paul often disagreed, as they sought to get Christians to return to living under the law of the Old Testament. In so doing, they were shifting followers of Christ back into a lifestyle of spiritual bondage. In response to these influences by the Judaizers, Paul wrote the letter we now call Galatians, as well as other passages of Scripture to address the retreat being encouraged back to the Mosaic law as a standard for Christian living.

In Galatians 2:4 Paul called these Judaizers, "The false brethren . . . who had sneaked in to spy out our liberty which we have in Christ Jesus, in order to bring us into bondage."

> IT IS POSSIBLE FOR LIBERATED BELIEVERS TO LIVE LIKE SLAVES IN BONDAGE AGAIN.

Clearly, from this passage and others, we see that it is possible for liberated believers to live like slaves in bondage again. Just because the gift of grace has been given doesn't automatically translate into its usage. God offers each of us, through the sacrifice of the cross, the enjoyment of His grace, but He doesn't force it on anyone. Yet to those who will accept and embrace it, it is the fuel for an on-fire kind of life.

Flying on the Trapeze

In years past, I took my kids to a trapeze show. It was their first time to ever see such daring feats and they sat there breathtaken. I also sat amazed watching the dexterity and the timing of the trapeze artists. We gasped at the near-misses and applauded the successes.

The show that we attended, like most trapeze shows, had a net spread tightly underneath them. This is in case anyone did fall by mistake. If they did, they could simply jump up and bounce back to the trapeze or walk to the ladder and climb back up. Knowing this reality empowered them to go higher, risk more, dare deeper, and perform better than they ever could have without it.

In Christ through the cross, we live on the trapeze. The whole world should be able to watch and say, "Look how they live, how they love one another. Look how well the husbands treat their wives. And aren't they the best workers in the marketplace and offices, the best neighbors, the best students?"

That is to live on the trapeze, being on display to those around you because of the confidence that comes through the security of Christ. What happens when we slip? The net is surely there. The blood of our Lord Jesus Christ has provided forgiveness for all of our sins, mistakes, and unwise choices. Both the net and the ability to stay on the trapeze are works of God's grace. Of course, we cannot be continually sleeping on the net. If that is the case, I doubt whether that person is a trapezist. But the gift of grace ought to affect how we live—how we love, how we hope, and how we serve God through a life of abandon to Him.

Being a Fool . . . without the Grace of the Cross

A trapeze artist would be a fool to refuse the net and return to a performance routine based on his or her own perfection alone. Mainly because no trapezist is ever completely perfect. Likewise, Paul uses this same harsh term for believers in Jesus Christ who are trying to live out the victorious Christian life apart from the grace of the cross. They are "foolish."

He starts out in Galatians 1 by addressing the situation boldly, "I am amazed that you are so quickly deserting Him who called you by the grace of Christ, for a different gospel; which is really not another; only there are some who are disturbing you and want to distort the gospel of Christ" (vv. 6–7).

Paul then continues in chapter 3 with what might be one of the greatest, yet most underutilized, passages in all of Scripture,

You foolish Galatians, who has bewitched you, before whose eyes Jesus Christ was publicly portrayed as crucified? This is the only thing I want to find out from you: did you receive the Spirit by the works of the Law, or by hearing with faith? Are you so foolish? Having begun by the Spirit, are you now being perfected by the flesh? Did you suffer so many things in vain—if indeed it was in vain? So then, does He who provides you with the Spirit and works miracles among you, do it by the works of the Law, or by hearing with faith? (vv. 3:1–5)

Here Paul states what legalism is in an interrogative format. He asks pointedly (as I paraphrase), "How did you get saved? Did you get saved by keeping the Ten Commandments? Did you get saved by being better than your next-door neighbor? Did you get saved by trying and trying and trying? Because if that's how you got saved, then you aren't really saved. No one is saved by works of righteousness. No one is saved by being a good man or a good woman. No one is saved by keeping the law. Because no one can do it perfectly. You are saved by grace."

Essentially Paul wants to remind the believers in Galatia—as well as us—that each person receives spiritual salvation apart from their own effort. Seeking to mix human effort with grace is akin to seeking to mix oil with water. The two just can't merge by virtue of their own component natures.

After bringing this reality to light, Paul adds a question on top of a question. He proceeds to state that if it was impossible for you or me or the people in the church at Galatia to get saved apart from grace, then why have they become so foolish as to believe that what was good enough to get them started is not good enough to keep them going? What makes us think that the Christ who set us free by the Spirit is now asking us to revert back to the law in order to stay free and live victoriously? That's backward thinking, at its best. That is legalism.

Legalism Defined

What then is legalism? Legalism is that system of rules and regulations that govern and define your identity and spiritual living entirely on your performance. It makes keeping rules the basis of your spiritual victory. It says, "You are what you do."

Keep in mind what legalism is not, though. Legalism is not the absence of rules or laws. We could not function without rules, guidelines, and laws. Legalism involves an inaccurate perception of and attitude toward those rules, thus attributing to rules a power that rules were never created to have.

In fact, legalism goes so far as to give rules a greater authority than even God Himself. For example, a quick look at the life of Elijah reveals God's authority over His rules. In one situation, Elijah found himself desperate, starving, and alone in the wilderness. In 1 Kings we are given a picture of what happened during that time as it says that the Lord Himself spoke to Elijah, "Go away from here and turn eastward, and hide yourself by the brook Cherith, which is east of the JorDaniel It shall be that you will drink of the brook, and I have commanded the ravens to provide for you there" (1 Kings 17:3–4). Elijah did as God said and God instructed the ravens to bring him bread and meat in the morning, as well as bread and meat in the evening.

At first glance, that's a very powerful and affirming story of God's provision for His servant Elijah. But deeper study of the Scripture reminds us that ravens, under the Law, were "abhorrent, not to be eaten" (Leviticus 11:13–15). Yet God has Elijah accept food from these unclean birds.

Not long after the situation of God superseding His own law to provide for Elijah, God sent him to a widow in Zerapheth, where she prepared food for him to eat and showed faith in him as a prophet—that is until her son died. Then the widow's faith waned, and Elijah was left to address the death of her son with God alone. The Bible tells us that he carried the dead son to the upper room, prayed before the Lord and "then he stretched himself upon the child three times" (1 Kings 17:21). The child returned to life.

Again, this is a great story of a great miracle. But what is often left out in the preaching of this story is the reality that Elijah—a prophet of God—under the Law would be considered unclean to touch a dead body (Numbers 9:6; 19:13), let alone carry one up the stairs and then stretch himself out on it three times. God didn't strike Elijah dead for his act of faith on behalf of this boy; rather God revived the boy.

It certainly isn't common practice for God to operate outside of His laws or desire us to do so, but these two very bold and known occurrences are just two of several others that occur in Scripture. And they are enough for us to know that the God we serve is greater than the Law. That doesn't do away with the law, by any means. But what it should do is open your eyes to see where your primary focus should truly be—that is, on the God of the Law, not the Law of God.

The Problems with Legalism

Having a list of rules that you follow is not the way that you find liberty and victory in the Christian life. It corrupts your motivation and in so doing negates the very actions of keeping the law. A guilt-motivated system forces a commitment on you that you will, at some point, fall short of upholding. What's worse, it births pride in you for what you do keep in the law and thereby reduces or eliminates the gratitude within you to the Spirit who makes all things possible.

Legalism sets your alarm clock to spend time in the Word while your mind is elsewhere. It puts you on your knees to pray when your heart refuses to bow as well. It creates a charade of outward activity and actions surrounding a shallow shell of resentment. What develops is an attitude based on rules and not on relationship.

Suppose you were married and your husband had a checklist to measure the state of your marriage. Not only did he give you this checklist but he expected you to carry it around with you all day. The checklist gave you the things that you were responsible to do, such as washing, cooking, cleaning, talking to him, organizing, and much more. As you did each item, you got to check it off—only to have to check it off again the next day and the next.

I've not known anyone with a checklist like that in a marriage relationship, but I can honestly say that I don't think there would be much warmth in such a marriage. Because whenever a marriage relationship is reduced to a checklist, the couple has turned what was intended to be communal and loving into something that is merely legalistic in nature, thus missing the point of marriage—marriage is to be a loving response, not a series of acts of necessity.

When you measure your Christian life by a checklist, you've missed the point of your relationship with God as well. Not because the things on the list are bad. It's just that having a list doesn't accomplish the heart of why those things on the list exist. God knows our hearts better than we even know them ourselves, and what creates true intimacy in our lives with Him are actions motivated by love. Through these actions, we unearth the greater power of His intimacy and care. Not through actions motivated by the law.

Under Two Masters

In my four decades of ministry, legalism has been one of the gravest ills to plague congregants and those responding to our national radio and speaking ministry. It is a constant drip that far too many still suffer under. Perhaps people seek rules to feel safe, proud, or vindicated; I'm not sure. Whatever the reason, Paul says clearly in his letter to the Romans that when we live our lives by the law, we serve another master apart from Jesus Christ. He writes, "For sin shall not be master over you, for you are not under law but under grace" (Romans 6:14).

Paul continues to illustrate the point of two masters in Romans 7 when he compares the mastery of law and the mastery of Christ to that of marriage. The illustration is poignant and graphic when writes:

Or do you not know, brethren (for I am speaking to those who know the law), that the law has jurisdiction over a person as long as he lives? For the married woman is bound by law to her husband while he is living; but if her husband dies, she is released from the law concerning the husband. So then, if while her husband is living she is joined to another man, she shall be called an adulteress; but if her husband dies, she is free from the law, so that she is not an adulteress though she is joined to another man.

Therefore, my brethren, you also were made to die to the Law through the body of Christ, so that you might be joined to another, to Him who was raised from the dead, in order that we might bear fruit for God. (vv. 1–4)

Paul uses this detailed situation of a married man and woman to show how trying to live as a Christian based on law rather than grace makes you a spiritual adulterer. This is because you can't live as a believer under two masters, just like a woman can't live as a wife under two masters. I know we've used marriage as a backdrop for understanding legalism versus grace throughout this chapter, but it is such an ideal illustrator simply because it is the closest covenantal union we have in the physical, tangible realm. So I'm going to use it again. If a woman was married to a man who was very rules-oriented and list-driven, she might find herself frustrated. However, after a few years her husband, whom we'll call Jeff, dies. At that point, under Paul's example, the woman is free from the bonds of Jeff.

When this woman later marries another man, whom we'll call Dave, he inspires and adores her, and she finds herself doing things for Dave simply because she wants to. Yet she still brings into the new relationship a lot of that old thinking that Jeff placed in her.

This woman has had Jeff mounted and stuffed in the easy chair in their new home. She just can't let go of the past. This happens even though Dave is able to draw out her emotions unlike Jeff ever could.

"I love you," she tells Dave one day, "but you've got to understand that I've lived with Jeff for so long that I still keep him nearby."

It goes without saying that Dave is not too keen on this situation. His wife either needs to give up her old love altogether, or stay with her old, dead love. To be free with her new love, she needs to bury Jeff.

Many of us in Christendom have been married to a rule-oriented

Jeff. We were raised on Jeff, who makes our lives predictable and formulaic. His rules approach to the Christian life often makes our actions mere habits. When Jesus Christ and His cross appear, we should be able to break free from Jeff. We can't bring a living Savior into our hearts, minds, and souls without burying the rules of Jeff. Jesus will not make His abode where a dead man still calls the shots.

The Virtues—and Limits—of God's Law

Paul's point is not that the law is bad. In fact, he comes right out and says the opposite in Romans 7: "So then, the law is holy, and the commandment is holy and righteous and good" (v. 12). The Law is good, but legalism brings the wrong viewpoint to the law. So why does the law exist? I'll start by telling you why it doesn't exist. It doesn't exist to make you better. Rather, the law exists for you to know what's wrong with you.

You wouldn't know lying was wrong unless someone told you it was wrong. The law is like a speed sign on the expressway that says 70 mph. That's the law. The law doesn't make you drive 70 mph; it just tells you that is the law and it validates that fact whenever a policeman pulls you over for exceeding the speed limit.

The law is like an X-ray machine that can reveal what is going on inside of you that others, or even yourself, could not discern by simply looking. The X-ray machine isn't designed to fix what is going on inside of you; it's only designed to show you what is there. Neither is the law itself designed to fix your sin nature and the vices with which you personally struggle. But it is designed to reveal them to you. If, by chance, you look to the law to fix what's wrong by creating lists that make it the goal to simply not carry out an action, apart from a change on the inside within your spirit, mind, and heart, then you will be setting yourself up for ultimate failure. The law, like an X-ray machine, is not created to fix that which it is created to reveal. That is the work of the Holy Spirit.

Paul speaks a lot on these issues of law, grace, and the Spirit. But one place in particular makes another—and for us a final—point on this all-important subject of legalism. Paul writes, "Not that we are adequate in ourselves to consider anything as coming from ourselves, but our adequacy is from God, who also made us adequate as servants of a new covenant, not of the letter but of the Spirit; for the letter kills, but the Spirit gives life" (2 Corinthians 3:5–6). Once again Paul points out the difference between the Spirit and the law. Essentially, he says that the law kills but the Spirit gives life.

Friend, the law is there to reveal the areas in your life where you are falling short of God's standard for you. But the Holy Spirit's work within you—through an abiding relationship with Jesus Christ because of His death on the cross—will both motivate you and enable you to live a life that pleases the Lord. Through the cross, the Spirit also will give you an abundance of personal goodness, satisfaction, peace, and every good thing.

The cross was God's way of introducing to our sinful selves the solution to the law: the ongoing work of the Holy Spirit in each of us.

PART 3

THE POWER
OF THE CROSS

9

THE STABILITY

MY SON, ANTHONY JR., had the opportunity to perform as a guest on NBC's hit program *The Voice* several years ago. Through that experience, he was able to publicly testify about Jesus Christ, as well as be a witness to those around him. He won the audition, chosen by Christina Aguilera, and later went to Universal Studios in California to compete in the first "battle round" against another audition winner. His two sisters, his mom, and I were in the audience along with about seven hundred others, while a national TV audience in the millions listened to the singers.

As we watched Christina struggle on who to choose, I whispered a simple prayer. "Lord, Your will be done." Needless to say I was disappointed when Anthony wasn't selected but at the same time proud of him for his performance and the great character he demonstrated when the decision was announced. I was thrilled to be at the whole event and to see Anthony perform at such a high level.

For the earlier audition round, all contestants were assigned a song to sing. The song chosen for Anthony was "What's Going On" by Marvin Gaye.

Gaye penned the lyrics of this song some time back, summarizing a number of the negative realities of the world, and asking the question,

"What's going on?" He knew that something was amiss, bringing havoc in many dimensions of society.

A similar question is often posed to me by members of our church. They approach me, each with their own burden, and ask, "Pastor, what's going on? What is happening?" For many in American society, a day does not go by where there does not seem to be more chaos, confusion, and uncertainty.

This uncertainty doesn't occur just in our society. Many people living overseas look at their own personal struggles and raise the question, "What is happening in my life?"

In Hebrews 12, the author writes to Jewish Christians who are raising the very same question. Jerusalem is about to be besieged by the Roman general Titus and his army. The temple will soon be destroyed and the dark clouds of despair have gathered on the horizon. Later in the book of Hebrews, we learn that some have been imprisoned (13:3), while others have had their property confiscated.

As you might imagine, in the midst of such pain, turmoil, and uncertainty, the question emerges: How should a person respond to the chaos ensuing all around? In this setting Christians are questioning their faith and their beliefs, asking where is the power, stability, and authority that they want to experience.

To be honest, the culture of the present century differs only slightly from that existing when Hebrews was written. Events still are shaking people's resolve. At the beginning of this century, terrorism reared its ugly head, changing the way we live and view ourselves and the world. The great recession of 2007 to 2009 affected all Americans to some degree, and some Americans to a devastating degree. People have lost their retirements and the security of their futures. The opportunity to find a decent paying job, or life as we once knew it, has alluded many more ever since.

Now, in the second decade of this century, family life seems in disarray. Same-sex marriages are being legalized—and most recently by the US Supreme Court—and even endorsed by the highest office in our land. Divorce continues to shatter both people's present and their future. In addition, psychological trauma is at an all-time high. Antidepressants, mood-stabilizing drugs, and antianxiety pills are prescribed, as more people find it difficult to cope with the realities of modern life. Much has happened in the last few years to place our nation on the precipice of uncertainty.

In short, we have been shaken.

In the midst of a similar environment, the author of Hebrews offers a word about life after the cross. He does so through a distinct contrast between Mount Sinai and Mount Zion. On Mount Sinai God spoke to Israel in the Old Testament. Yet on Mount Zion we are introduced to the new covenant given to us by the blood of Jesus Christ shed on the cross. It is under the tenants and truths of Mount Zion that we find ourselves today. It is precisely because of the cross of Jesus Christ that we no longer live in light of Mount Sinai.

The writer of Hebrews reminds us of what life under Mount Sinai was like when he writes,

> For you have not come to a mountain that can be touched and to a blazing fire, and to darkness and gloom and whirlwind, and to the blast of a trumpet and the sound of words which sound was such that those who heard begged that no further word be spoken to them. For they could not bear the command, "If even a beast touches the mountain, it will be stoned." And so terrible was the sight, that Moses said, "I am full of fear and trembling." (Hebrews 12:18–21)

In order to fully realize and maximize the power and stability of the cross, we need to recall what life was like before Christ's willing sacrifice. When God had come down to Sinai and spoken prior to giving the Ten Commandments, it was a sight to behold as the mountain began to smoke and quake. God's presence shook the entire mountain so much that the people ran away, did not want to listen, and even Moses himself trembled.

THE HOLINESS OF GOD IS AWESOME. YET ON THE CROSS, JESUS CHRIST OFFERED HIMSELF AS [OUR] MEDIATOR.

The holiness of God and the perfection of God are so awesome that to even be near Him shakes things up. Yet on the cross Jesus Christ has given us access to the God of the universe. On the cross, Jesus Christ offered Himself as the mediator between God and man. It was there that He initiated the new covenant.

As the writer of Hebrews continues, he tells us about this access and mediation. We learn Mount Sinai is not our mountain. Mount Zion is our mountain. We read:

> But you have come to Mount Zion and to the city of the living God, the heavenly Jerusalem, and to myriads of angels, to the general assembly and church of the firstborn who are enrolled in heaven, and to God, the Judge of all, and to the spirits of the righteous made perfect, and to Jesus, the mediator of a new covenant, and to the sprinkled blood, which speaks better than the blood of Abel. (vv. 22–24)

These verses declare that you have been moved to a new city, and you are living in a new realm. You are not living at Mount Sinai where there is trembling and insecurity. That is not your home as a believer in Jesus Christ because of what Jesus accomplished at the cross. The blood of Jesus Christ has orchestrated a new covenant in which Jesus serves as mediator between you and God. Through Christ's atoning blood, a new covenant exists whereby Jesus is covenantally committed to you.

Keep in mind this new covenant is based on blood, "which speaks better than the blood of Abel" (12:24). Remember that Cain shed Abel's blood, and in response Abel's blood called out from the ground, crying for justice (Genesis 4:10). When God heard the cry for justice, He responded. This is because the blood spoke judgment.

But the writer of Hebrews declares that the blood shed at the cross mediated an entirely different arrangement with God. Christ's blood in the new covenant called for mercy and commitment.

Therefore, when things in your life seem messed up, shaken, or are uncertain, you need to view God and His relationship with you through the lens of this new arrangement—the cross—or you will get it all wrong.

When Life Is Unstable

In the final section of Hebrews 12 we receive insight into how we are to view God when our lives begin to unravel and become unstable:

See to it that you do not refuse Him who is speaking. For if those did not escape when they refused him who warned them on earth, much less will we escape who turn away from Him who warns from heaven. And His voice *shook* the earth then, but now He has promised, saying, "Yet once more I will *shake* not only the earth, but also the heaven." This expression, "Yet once more," denotes the removing of those things which can be *shaken*, as of created things, so that those things which cannot be *shaken* may remain. (vv. 25–27, italics added)

If you are struggling today, please note that in this passage the author repeatedly uses the word "shaken" or a derivative therein. If your world has been shaken, or your personal life, emotions, finances, career, or anything else has been shook up, you are not alone. If it has become difficult for you to sleep peacefully at night, then you know your life has been shaken. If it has become difficult for you to focus like you used to, you know your world has become shaken. If it has become difficult to find the happiness in the things that used to make you happy, your world has been shaken. At times you may feel afraid, angry, unstable, and insecure.

When any of that happens, as a believer in Jesus Christ, remember that you are a part of the new covenant. You are a part of a group of people uniquely attached to the cross of Christ, and all that it entails. Because of this, God has a different end goal for the shaking. In addition, because of the cross, you are now enabled to hear and draw close to Him.

God's goal is not simply to announce His presence and lead you to fear, awe, and trembling to such a degree that you beg Him to leave because you cannot bear it. Rather it is to announce His presence in order to draw you close to Him. He has something that He wants to not only tell you but also to do in you. Remember we read, "See to it that you do not refuse Him who is speaking" (Hebrews 12:25).

God is talking and He has something very important to say.

When I was a young child and an enormous thunderstorm would develop outside our house, my grandmother would always make me turn off the television or the radio because, as she put it, "God is talking." So we children would all sit there in the silence as "God talked." Actually, it was just thunder, but the principle holds true when things become shaky in your life. God is talking and He wants you to listen.

Today when there is bad weather or a forecast of bad weather, families will frequently turn on car radios or turn to weather websites for the latest weather report. During those times, we typically give the weather reporter our undivided focus. We tune in because things are starting to get shaky.

Friend, when God allows or even causes things to be shaken nationally, locally, or even personally, do not "refuse Him who is speaking." God is talking. In fact, the shakier things get, the louder He is speaking.

Painful Scenarios

I have four children and, at the time of this writing, twelve grandchildren. Having experienced, to some degree at least, the births of sixteen babies over the years, I can say without hesitation that a mother's act of labor is an intense, painful, shaky experience. Anguish manifests itself because the baby is speaking. Now, the baby is speaking indirectly, of course, yet the baby is definitely sending a message. The message? "I want out!" When the baby in the womb starts to speak that message, everyone listens.

It is a powerful message of separation, of an impending separation of the baby from the mother. That removal process hurts. In fact, as the pain intensifies, the closer the mother is to the separation and change.

Keep in mind, the separation is good news in a bad situation. The bad situation is that it is painful. It hurts. We can't deny that it hurts. But the good news is that there is new life about to be made known. It's time to manifest healthy change.

When God was ready to do something special—and wonderful—throughout Scripture, it would be introduced through a painful scenario.

God would either allow or create anguish or physical pain in order to introduce the new situation. Frequently, when God is ready to do something new in our lives, He knows that we are not ready for it. We are too set in our ways, tied to our past, or attached to a wrong way of thinking, and God must evoke a change within us before the new can occur. Because we are not ready, He makes us ready. A separation to what we previously depended on must occur so that we will not only look to Him but be able to see Him.

A classic example is when the Israelites were seemingly cornered at the Red Sea. God blocked them in and there was no way out. They had Pharaoh on one side and the Red Sea on the other, and so they found themselves in an uncertain situation. All they could see in every direction they looked was death.

The Israelites would have never seen God do the miraculous if they had not been positioned to such a degree that they needed the miraculous. God had to force the issue with the Israelites by creating and allowing such turbulence in their lives so that He could birth the next thing that He wanted to reveal to them about Himself.

> GOD WANTS TO DISCONNECT YOU FROM THE THINGS, THOUGHTS, OR PEOPLE OF THIS WORLD ORDER SO THAT HE CAN REVEAL TO YOU ETERNAL THINGS.

In shaking things up, or in allowing painful scenarios to occur in our lives, God is essentially eroding one realm—the temporal—to expose us to another realm—the eternal. He must shake us loose from the possessions, beliefs, or even people that we are too attached to in order to take us to the place He wants us to be.

God does this by creating discontinuity, disconnection, and destabilization in our lives. This, in turn, is designed to remove us from our loyalty to earth—and the ways of earth—so that we can witness the movement of heaven and the new covenant brought to us through the cross.

When God either allows or creates discontinuity in your life, He is speaking. He is saying something particularly about His new covenant with you. He is saying that He wants to disconnect you from the things, thoughts, or people of this world order so that He can reveal to you eternal things. As long as you are too dependent on anything other than God and His relationship with you, you are not hearing Him. That means He must continue to turn up the heat in your life.

You only feel the heat as He seeks to reveal to you your attachment to things of temporal value, rather than eternal value. On the ground during an earthquake, you are going to feel the shaking and trembling of the earth. However, if you are in an airplane flying above the shaking quake, you won't feel a thing. This is because you are no longer attached to that which is shaking. From above you can see the quake for what it is, a passing, temporary occurrence. By means of the cross, God wants to flow into and through you the blessings of the new covenant, but in order to do so He must disconnect you from that which is inconsistent with this covenant and the relationship that you are to be having with Him.

How can we be in the airplane when the shaking comes, riding out the tremors of life? Essentially, God wants to remove anything that does not add to His relationship with and His purpose for you. He removes that which can be removed, leaving you with our steady, sturdy foundation—your relationship with Him through the cross of Christ. Only it will remain steady. We read earlier about this when it said, "'Yet once more,' denotes the removing of those things which can be shaken, as of created things, so that those things which cannot be shaken may remain" (Hebrews 12:27).

The phrase "Yet once more" references the book of Haggai, in which the prophet spoke of God's statement that He would shake the nations in order to restore His glory in His temple. We read, "For thus says the Lord of hosts, 'Once more in a little while, I am going to shake the heavens and the earth, the sea also and the dry land. I will shake all the nations; and they will come with the wealth of all nations, and I will fill this house with glory,' says the Lord of hosts" (Haggai 2:6–7).

God had told Haggai He would shake things up in order to transfer things over. An easy way to get a picture of this is by comparing it to a child's piggy bank. The child's piggy bank would need to be shaken and shaken in order to get out the valuable items from within it. God said He would "shake" things up in order to shake something loose from one realm and deliver it to another, His own.

An Unshakeable Kingdom

This would happen at the cross. There the blood of Christ would mediate a new arrangement—a new realm—that God has with every believer, as well as with His church. That new arrangement is called the new covenant. Yet in order for this new covenant to manifest itself in your life, God needs to first disconnect you from the illegitimate blockages in the arteries of your spirit. He needs to remove your attachment and dependency on that which is not Him, those things that stand in the way of your relationship to Him.

Some of my greatest memories in my life have come out of crises where heaven had to step in because earth couldn't fix it. By "earth" I mean the program, thoughts, and processes of this world. In those times I learned firsthand that whatever I had previously depended on, even if it was myself, could be shaken. Yet the one thing that remained constant throughout, and that was able to eventually come in and solve the situation—or if it was not solved could stabilize me within the situation—was God. In the book of Hebrews we read that God shakes things in order to remove what can be shaken because what He offers through the cross is unshakeable. It is dependable, strong, and stable.

So Hebrews concludes, "Therefore, since we receive *a kingdom which cannot be shaken*, let us show gratitude, by which we may offer to God an acceptable service with reverence and awe; for our God is a consuming fire" (12:28–29, italics added).

To each believer the cross of Jesus Christ transforms what can be shaken into an unshakeable kingdom. You have received entrance into a kingdom that cannot be shaken. Friend, if you are only looking at the stock market pages, the banking system, your job, coworkers, family members, health, relationships, or that which you can see, you will be shaken.

Yet if you fix your eyes on the stability of the cross of Jesus Christ, you cannot be shaken. This is because you are operating with a different King, a different authority than the world. When you feel like your world is falling apart, make sure you don't refuse to listen to God at that time because He is speaking to you. He is trying to pry you loose from what He knows cannot offer you long-term peace, wisdom, or stability. When your world is crumbling all around you, if you will keep your eyes on Jesus Christ and the promise of the new covenant that He has given you through the cross, you will not crumble along with it.

The Scarlet Cord

One of my favorite Bible stories takes place on the wall of Jericho. It is not about Joshua and his army marching around Jericho and the walls falling down but about what happened to one portion of that wall—a portion that remained in place.

While everything crumbled and shook around and in Jericho that day, the house where a woman named Rahab lived remained intact. Rahab's home was located in the outer portion of the Jericho wall (Joshua 2:15). When she had earlier welcomed the spies into her home and hid them from her own government, she aligned herself with the Israelites and their covenantal relationship with God. So even though the kingdom of which she was physically a part—Jericho—fell apart, her home and her family within it were safe (6:22–23). This is because she had aligned herself with another King from an unshakeable kingdom and had placed herself under the covering and covenant of God.

The Jericho wall did fall, except for one piece of it where a prostitute named Rahab had placed a scarlet rope outside her window, showing her alignment with the one true God.

On the cross, Jesus' life became our scarlet rope aligning each of us who place our faith in Him with the new covenant. While things around you may become shaky, when you fix your eyes on Jesus, you will remember the promise of His covenant and that you belong to an unshakeable kingdom.

Our Foundation and Stability in Life

In this life there will be trials. God will frequently use these trials to reveal to you what can be shaken so that it will also be removed from you. He is a jealous God, and as we saw earlier, "our God is a consuming fire."

Remember that the purpose of the sacrifice (consumed by fire) in Old Testament times was to render judgment and to achieve a purification between God and man. What Christ did on the cross was act on our behalf in light of God as a "consuming fire." He is our foundation and the stability of our lives.

Therefore, when things heat up in your life, God is not bringing judgment on you. He is not trying to chase you away. Yes, He may be disciplining you because God disciplines those whom He loves. Or He may also be trying to separate you from that which you should not be so entirely attached to or dependent upon. But He is not judging you to punish you. Christ took our punishment on the cross.

God has a goal in mind for the trials and pain that enter our lives, and that goal is to shift us into a daily experience of His unshakeable kingdom.

When you wake up in the morning and you need to wear a nice outfit to work or to church, you will often want to iron your clothes before putting them on. This is because you don't want wrinkled clothing to reflect you poorly to those around you. So you plug in your iron and let it get hot to the touch. Then you slowly move it back and forth over the wrinkles in your clothes.

Your clothes feel the heat, the pressure, and the sting of the iron. You aren't putting the hot iron on your clothes because you want to burn them. You are simply trying to improve them and return them to their intended look and for their best use.

As a consuming fire, God will allow heat in your life to separate you from that which does not bring Him glory. This is because He has chosen to wear you as a reflection of Himself to others, which is our best use in serving our Creator. God wants you to glorify Him through your life. He longs to bless you, but He wants to make sure you are capable of receiving that blessing in faith.

The cross has given you a new arrangement, with God placing you in a kingdom that does not shake in spite of the shaking all around you. Therefore, in the midst of what troubles you, as bad as it is or as strong as the labor pains may feel, trust Him. Listen to Him. Look to Him. Honor Him. Respond to Him. Have faith in Him. He is not trying to hurt you. He is simply trying to reveal to you the things in your life that are of no eternal value, and frequently of little temporal value as well.

The cross is your comfort. It is your reminder that what you are experiencing is not judgment. In fact, it is just the opposite. The trials in your life are there to reveal the treasure of the new covenant and the stability and permanence that comes with alignment under God. They are designed to release you from, or to have you release, that which can be shaken in order to grow and expand your experience with that which cannot be shaken—God and His kingdom.

10

THE DELIVERANCE

FOR AN EXPECTANT MOTHER, delivery means release from birth pains. For a hiker who falls into a deep ravine with no way out, delivery means a rope, a basket, and a helicopter overhead. For a Midwest farmer and his wife facing a twisting tornado, delivery means the cellar doors leading to the underground.

Most of us need to be delivered from something at some point in time. It is a rare human being who faces no struggle, no challenge, and carries no weakness within themselves. It may not be dramatic or a life-or-death situation. But deliverance always means to be set free or released. It may involve the removal of something that binds you from the external. Other times it will be the healing of an attitude or addiction that binds you.

In Romans 5, Paul sets forth the delivering power of the cross. He writes, "For while we were still helpless, at the right time Christ died for the ungodly. For one will hardly die for a righteous man; though perhaps for the good man someone would dare even to die. But God demonstrates His own love toward us, in that while we were yet sinners, Christ died for us" (vv. 6–8).

In other words, when there was nothing lovely about us, Christ died for us in order to demonstrate His love. When we were His enemies, He redeemed us. When we were in rebellion against Him, He drew us to Him. When we were on the other side of the tracks and had no concern for Him, He crossed over and made a way back. Knowing the worst about us, He gave His best for us.

A lot of people will talk about love, but God demonstrated it. Yet not only did He demonstrate it, He added something on top of it: deliverance. The following verses in Romans 5 give us a glimpse into the delivering power of the cross where we read,

> Much more then, having now been justified by His blood, we shall be saved from the wrath of God through Him. For if while we were enemies we were reconciled to God through the death of His Son, much more, having been reconciled, we shall be saved by His life. And not only this, but we also exult in God through our Lord Jesus Christ, through whom we have now received the reconciliation. (vv. 9–11)

In this passage, we uncover that those who have been justified by Christ's blood, trusting in Him as their personal Savior through faith in Christ alone for the forgiveness of their sins, receive something else. It is introduced by the words "much more."

But what is this "much more"?

Delivered from Hell and from Wrath

In order to unearth what "much more" is, we need to take a careful look at the word "saved" in verse 9. This word literally means to be rescued or delivered. When a person says, "I'm saved," they are saying that they have been delivered from something, or rescued from something. When a person accepts Jesus Christ as one's sin-bearer, he or she is saved from eternal separation from God, what the Bible calls hell. But what Paul refers to in this passage as the "much more" doesn't have to do with salvation from hell. Rather, Paul is saying that on top of our salvation from hell, we have also been saved from the wrath of God through Jesus' death.

So what does the wrath of God mean and what does it look like? To fully mine the meaning of this verse, we have to dig deep into a thorough study of theology. In Scripture, theology is often spoken of in two separate terms. There is the term "systematic theology" and then there is the term "biblical theology."

Students of systematic theology take a biblical truth, review everything the Bible says about the truth, and then organize those principles into a system. That's why it's called systematic theology. The problem is that you can't go to one place in the Bible that talks about a subject and locate everything that there is to be found on that subject. You have to go to different places, uncover what it says in context, and then bring it all together. You have to systematize it, or organize it, in order to understand all that you can about it.

For example, if you wanted to study the holiness of God, you can't just go to one verse, chapter, or even book. You have to look at each passage that discusses the holiness of God and compare the passages to one another in order to fully understand the holiness of God.

But there is a second theological approach to studying Scripture as well, called biblical theology. While systematic theology looks at all that the Bible says on any given subject, biblical theology limits itself to what that particular author would say about that subject. In other words, biblical theology only examines what is being explained in that particular context, or that particular book by that particular person. It is not concerned with scanning the entire Bible to determine everything it says about the subject.

This is why biblical theology typically serves as a prerequisite to systematic theology, because you first want to fully understand the context, book, and author pertaining to a particular subject. Then you bring that insight to the other places of Scripture speaking on the same subject, as you move deeper in developing a systematic approach to it.

For example, when you are looking to understand a particular term in biblical theology, you will look to see where and how the author used that term before in the very same book. Then you look at all of the ways he used that term in that book as well. If he hasn't provided the permission to change the meaning of the term, then you retain the same meaning that he implied when he first introduced the concept.

Keep in mind, all of this is contained within a particular book. You can't look at a term used in Romans and then hop over to Revelation and see how it is used there in order to understand what it means in Romans, not according to biblical theology. Rather, you look at the book of Romans to understand what that term means within the book of Romans.

So the question I introduced earlier, "What is the wrath of God?" can first be answered by applying the method of biblical theology to the term. Is Paul talking about hell with that phrase, or is he talking about something else? By going back to Romans 1 where Paul first introduces the term, we can discern that he is talking about something else. Let's do a quick review so that you can grasp this for yourself: "For the wrath of God is revealed from heaven against all ungodliness and unrighteousness of men who suppress the truth in unrighteousness because that which is known about God is evident within them; for God made it evident to them" (1:18–19).

Paul tells readers that the wrath of God is revealed from heaven. Then he goes on to clearly show us what the revelation of that wrath looks like when we read the remainder of that chapter. Take the time to read through verses 20–32 in their entirety, because the accurate interpretation of this phrase "the wrath of God" is foundational in understanding the delivering power of the cross:

For since the creation of the world His invisible attributes, His eternal power and divine nature, have been clearly seen, being understood through what has been made, so that they are without excuse. For even though they knew God, they did not honor Him as God or give thanks, but they became futile in their speculations, and their foolish heart was darkened. Professing to be wise, they became fools, and exchanged the glory of the incorruptible God for an image in the form of corruptible man and of birds and four-footed animals and crawling creatures.

Therefore God gave them over in the lusts of their hearts to impurity, so that their bodies would be dishonored among them. For they exchanged the truth of God for a lie, and worshiped and served the creature rather than the Creator, who is blessed forever. Amen.

For this reason God gave them over to degrading passions; for their women exchanged the natural function for that which is unnatural, and in the same way also the men abandoned the natural function of the woman and burned in their desire toward one another, men with men committing indecent acts and receiving in their own persons the due penalty of their error.

And just as they did not see fit to acknowledge God any longer, God gave them over to a depraved mind, to do those things which are not proper, being filled with all unrighteousness, wickedness, greed, evil; full of envy, murder, strife, deceit, malice; they are gossips, slanderers, haters of God, insolent, arrogant, boastful, inventors of evil, disobedient to parents, without understanding, untrustworthy, unloving, unmerciful;

and although they know the ordinance of God, that those who practice such things are worthy of death, they not only do the same, but also give hearty approval to those who practice them. (vv. 20–32)

Throughout this passage, Paul is unpacking for us what this term "wrath" means within the context that he is choosing to use it. He has connected it to what men and women are doing on earth and lists a number of things that were happening back then—and are also occurring today. The wrath Paul defines in response to mankind's disobedience and rebellion against God is a visible demonstration of displeasure. It is not merely saying that God is mad; wrath is God tangibly showing that He is mad. It is not just anger; it is anger on display. In other words, it's not a secret nor is it hidden. Just as God visibly demonstrated His love for us when He sacrificed His Son, Jesus Christ, on our behalf, wrath is a visible demonstration of God's displeasure.

Visible Demonstrations of God's Wrath

In several of the above verses, we can pick up on what this visible demonstration looks like:

Therefore God gave them over. (v. 24)
For this reason God gave them over. (v. 26)
And just as they did not see fit to acknowledge God any longer, God gave them over. (v. 28)

The wrath that Paul is defining for us in Romans 1 is not eternal separation from God in hell but rather it involves God turning people over to the natural repercussions of their sin. He has withheld His mercy and His grace, while allowing the consequences of sin to unfold. This is God's passive wrath, where He withdraws His covering and protection, allowing mankind to not only pursue their fleshly corruptions but to also incur the resultant consequences in their lives and relationshiPsalm

The combination of God removing His common grace along with opening the valve of sin's consequential flow is the wrath of God. It was experienced in Paul's day and it is also experienced in our day on many levels. Mankind chooses to rebel against God to such a degree that the Creator ultimately steps aside and says, "Go for it." And, as a result of the removal of His Spirit's restraint, the judgment of sin comes through the very ramifications of that sin itself.

AIDS (Acquired Immune Deficiency Syndrome) and the HIV infection that causes it are perfect examples of the passive wrath of God. In heterosexual, monogamous relationships, which are according to His principles of sexual morality and faithfulness, HIV does not occur. When men and women live under the rule of God, HIV will have no place among couples. However, when men and women choose to live alternatively to God's prescribed plan for marriage, His passive wrath allows for that which naturally comes as a result of sex with multiple partners. Similarly, AIDS among drug users (spread by dirty needles) reflects the consequences of breaking state and federal laws and ignoring those in authority.

Another example of this happened in the United States during the economic misdeeds that led to the Great Recession of 2008. Paul describes people "filled with greed" (1:29). Recall the greed from the consumers, bankers, and mortgage companies that accumulated upon itself until God allowed a national financial collapse. Many people bought homes they could not afford, prompted by mortgage lenders who lowered qualifying standards in order to make money. The lenders approved sub-prime mortgages that eventually contributed to a stock market collapse, a drop in home valuations, and thousands of home foreclosures. This financial collapse didn't happen simply because of bad financial management; rather it was also a result of divine judgment that opened the doors for the natural outgrowth of greed's results.

Clearly the wrath of God occurs when God removes His hands of mercy, thus allowing the consequences of sin to run wild.

Our Repentance, Christ's Intercession

This being so, we carry that definition into Romans 5:9–11, the key passage for this chapter. Paul wrote, "Much more then, having now been justified by His blood, we shall be saved from the wrath of God through Him" (v. 9). When you bring your sin to the cross and trust in the shed blood of Jesus Christ for forgiveness, the Deliverer not only pardons your sin for eternity but the life of Christ delivers you from the current outworkings of the consequences of your sin. That's the deliverance in history that Christ came to provide.

Why? Because whether you are a Christian or a non-Christian, you face the same physical and tangible consequences of sin. When Christians operate out of a spirit and mindset of envy, jealousy, evil, sexual licentiousness, and the like, they are inviting into their lives the same consequences as everyone else. The cross of Christ allows us to take our sin to Jesus, ask for His forgiveness, and seek His healing hand. Jesus can then deliver us from God's passive wrath.

That is why repentance is so important. Jesus Christ lives to make intercession for you. Not only does He intercede for you, but like a lead blocker in football, He deflects the enemy's attempts to defeat you. Satan is a master at leveraging and maximizing the effects and results of sin's consequences in our lives. He often twists these consequences with guilt and shame in order to make them even worse than they are on their own. But when you truly understand the sacrificial love of God on the cross, and come to Jesus in repentance for your sin, Jesus will open the way so you can make progress down the field of life. For you and me to fully realize the deliverance God has in store for us, we must bring our sins—whether they be attitudes, actions, or thoughts—and lay them at the foot of the cross.

When we live apart from the awareness and alignment under the cross, it creates distance between us and God. It's like the ever-shining sun of our earth: Even though the sun is always shining, we experience darkness (nighttime) several hours each day simply because our side of the planet has turned away from the sun. Darkness sets in when we are no longer facing the light. Similarly, when we turn from God by suppressing His truth, as written in Romans 5, then you experience the resulting darkness of no longer facing Him.

Of course, God is light. But when we position ourselves away from the light, we can walk into darkness. What the deliverance of the cross does is usher us back into the truth of God's standards, His love, and His mercy. It frees us from a life of bondage to the results of sin and its consequences in your life.

> TO FULLY REALIZE THE DELIVERANCE GOD HAS FOR US, WE MUST BRING OUR SINS AND LAY THEM AT THE FOOT OF THE CROSS.

That doesn't mean that you will never experience sin's consequences. God doesn't always deliver from everything, but what it does mean is that you will have positioned yourself to receive His best for you and for Him to cover you with both His grace and His mercy.

THE POWER OF THE CROSS

Confess and Believe

We've been looking at the book of Romans thus far to see the delivering power of the cross, but in Romans 10 we come to two verses that have confused a lot of people over the years. They read: "If you *confess* with your mouth Jesus as Lord, and *believe* in your heart that God raised Him from the dead, you will be saved; for with the heart a person believes, resulting in righteousness, and with the mouth he confesses, resulting in salvation" (vv. 9–10, italics added).

In these two verses Paul lists two things we must do to be *saved*: confess with our mouth and believe in our heart. The problem comes about because every other place in the New Testament that explains how to get saved tells us that we only have to do one thing: believe (John 3:16; John 5:24; Acts 16:31; Romans 4:5). Yet in Romans, we have to do a second thing. So either the Bible is contradicting itself, or this passage in Romans must mean something else.

The answer to that dilemma comes in the context of the passage. Paul is not instructing sinners on how to become saints in this passage. He is instructing saints on how to get delivered from present sins. You must believe on the Lord Jesus Christ to go to heaven, but you must confess the Lord Jesus Christ to get heaven to come to you.

Let me explain. When a person accepts Jesus Christ as their personal Savior (believe), Jesus' righteousness is immediately credited (imputed) to them as their righteousness. They are saved, in the eternal sense of the word. Yet when they make a public confession of Jesus Christ as their risen Lord, they receive His deliverance in the here and now, in history. Thus there is a direct relationship between the cross and the resurrection of Jesus Christ to God delivering His people from the death-dealing consequences of sin.

The word "saved" is the same word we've been looking at already regarding deliverance. The reason why a lot of people who are going to heaven are not seeing heaven join them in history is because they have believed but they have not confessed. They have placed their faith in Jesus Christ for the forgiveness of their sins. But they have not made an ongoing public confession, or declaration, of Him as their Lord— whether through word or deed.

Jesus Christ as Lord

In biblical days in Rome, Christians would be brought before the magistrates because these Christ followers were declaring Jesus as Lord in both speech and actions. The term "Lord" means supreme ruler or authority. The Roman authorities would attempt to get the Christians to declare Caesar as Lord, and deny Jesus as supreme ruler and authority. Believing in Jesus didn't get the Christians hung or tossed to the lions for sport; believing in Jesus as the rightful ruler and Lord did. There's a difference.

The reason we may not be seeing more of God's deliverance in our lives is because we have Jesus positioned as our Savior, but not as our Lord. We, the collective body of Christ, are not His slaves. Keep in mind that the job of a slave is do whatever the Master says to do.

Unfortunately today in the lives of many Christians, Jesus must compete with other masters. Yet Jesus is not willing to be one among many. He is not willing to be part of an association or club. Neither is He willing to be relegated as a personal assistant. Jesus as Lord means that Jesus is to be *the* supreme ruler and master. He calls the shots, and He is to be acknowledged in everything that is done.

The problem is that too many people want a Savior on the cross but don't want the Lord who rose again. Because of this, many Christians today are experiencing the result of denying Christ publicly. They are likewise being denied by Christ before God, the Father. How does this denial occur? Several other passages in both the Old and New Testaments will give us insight. Let's read them first:

For whoever will call on the name of the Lord will be saved. (Romans 10:13)

Paul, called as an apostle of Jesus Christ by the will of God . . . , to those who have been sanctified in Christ Jesus, saints by calling, with all who in every place call on the name of our Lord Jesus Christ, their Lord and ours. (1 Corinthians 1:1–2)

And it will come about that whoever calls on the name of the Lord will be delivered. (Joel 2:32)

These are just a few passages, but from them we can see clearly that those being addressed are already saved from an eternal standpoint. They are "saints by calling." The word "deliverance" doesn't mean salvation in view of eternity. In the context of these passages, and the passage we read earlier in Romans 10, deliverance is God's help in history. Calling on the name of the Lord invokes heaven to join you down here.

Let me explain how this works. Let's say I was to call on God to deliver me from something that I was struggling with, or a circumstance that I was facing. It was entirely too much for me to bear or overcome on my own, and I needed to be delivered. So I call on the name of the Lord. When that happens, God, the Father, turns to Christ, the Son, and says, "Son, Tony Evans just called on Me because he wants to be rescued from a particular situation. What do You say?"

Jesus then responds, "Father, Tony Evans never wants to bring up My name in public. He's embarrassed about his association with Me. He does not want Me to influence his decision making. Whenever religion comes up, he changes the subject. He'll use your name, 'God,' but He won't ever mention Mine, 'Jesus Christ.' He's never willing to share his faith with anyone. So if You answer his request for deliverance, all You are doing is giving him a

> TO EXPERIENCE HEAVEN'S POWER ON EARTH, A PERSON MUST BE WILLING TO CONFESS JESUS CHRIST AS LORD.

new opportunity to deny Me. Based on that, I would recommend that You deny His request since He denies Me."

Now, hopefully none of that is true of me in the literal sense, since I've made it my life mission to declare Jesus Christ publicly. But you get the point. You can call on the name of the Lord all you want for deliverance, but according to Romans 10:9–10, if you have not also confessed the name of the Lord that you call on, your request could be denied. To experience heaven's authority and power on earth, a person must be willing to confess Jesus Christ as Lord, publicly in what they say and do.

You believe on Him for eternal salvation. You confess Him publicly for deliverance in history. Both His investment and His involvement in your life hinges upon your public declaration through both words and actions that He is Lord. Paul told Timothy boldly, "Therefore do not be ashamed of the testimony of our Lord" (2 Timothy 1:8).

If for no other practical reason than accessing the power of deliverance on earth, you must establish and declare Jesus Christ as Lord of your life. You must open your mouth publicly and let others know through what you say and through what you do that He is your Lord and Master—that you are not ashamed to be associated with Him and under Him. He is seated at the right hand of God in the heavenlies, as are you through His redemption on the cross. His blood has established the new covenant under which you are to align your life and world in order to receive its full covenantal covering and protection.

You've probably heard someone say, "I plead the blood." What they are talking about is the blood of the covenant. However, the way you plead the blood of the covenant is not simply by saying some magical words. You plead the blood of the covenant by being under the terms of the covenant—by making Jesus Christ Lord of your life and ruler of your world.

11

THE REMEMBRANCE

I'M A PREACHER BY nature. God created me with an innate passion and desire to preach His Word. I've been preaching as far back as my teenage years, whether that meant climbing onto the back of a parked truck to preach on a street corner or breaking down the Scripture in small tent revivals. It didn't matter where or how long—I have always longed and loved to preach.

Sunday morning, without a doubt, is the highlight of my week. We have two services at the church I've pastored for nearly four decades, and a typical sermon will last anywhere from forty-five minutes to an hour. The entire service is about two hours. Yet despite how much I love to preach and pour myself into the message delivered each week, I can honestly say that the sermon is not the most important part of the service.

Yes, the sermon is important, instructional, and intended to be inspirational, but it definitely is not the most important part of the service. Neither is the singing, even though worship through music certainly is a key component that fosters relational intimacy with God. The most essential element of the Sunday morning service is Communion. In fact, we celebrate it every week. Unfortunately, the most important part of our service is also one of the least understood and most underutilized in all of Christendom.

The practice of Communion is key to unlocking God's unique presence and power in each of our lives. It takes us back to the cross where Jesus died. As such, it ought to be an integral part of our communion with God, and it ought to take us deeper in our relationship with Him through every experience. However, most of us don't truly grasp the significance of Communion and therefore fail to maximize its value.

Far too many consume the wafer and drink the contents of the cup, all within the mindset of a generalized, atmospheric understanding of Communion, thus merely going through the motions. It's not that there is no sincerity. It's not that the confession doesn't occur, or that gratitude isn't given. It is just that we don't always fully manifest the true meaning of Communion in our hearts and minds, and so we end up at a loss for how to approach it any differently than we've ever done since the time we were first saved. After all, biblical teaching on the cross and its connection to Communion isn't a typical Sunday morning message or Bible study subject.

What's more, at a number of churches Communion is not done regularly but rather it is reserved for special occasions only. And then even when it is done, it isn't always wrapped with a time of reflection and meditation on the entirety of the truth it conveys but only on the highlights of that truth.

If we as believers were to thoroughly understand and apply the purpose and power of the Lord's Table—Communion, the Lord's Supper (sometimes called the Eucharist—it would be a transformative experience in our lives. And I don't mean transformative simply in the nature of our hearts toward the Lord, but also in the access to the authority and power that Christ on the cross has accomplished for us, and intends for us to benefit from in the nitty-gritty of our daily lives.

What a Sermon Can't Fix

Without a doubt, both our congregants and listeners to our radio and television ministries deal with issues that are intense, complex, and often unrelenting. So many people come to church, carrying things that a sermon alone can't fix. They come in broken at a level that inspiration can't mend. They need something bigger, stronger, and more powerful that will affect whatever it is that engulfs them. Perhaps you need something like that too.

This is exactly what Communion is designed to do.

Paul's letter to the church at Corinth sets the backdrop for our discussion on this subject and highlights how Communion—the remembrance of Jesus' death on the cross—can impact us for good. While writing to the believers about topics such as marriage and community, Paul launched into the best-known passage on Communion. Because it is so well-known, it is easy to skim over the words and lose sight of their full meaning. I invite you to read it once again, this time slowly.

> For I received from the Lord that which I also delivered to you, that the Lord Jesus in the night in which He was betrayed took bread; and when He had given thanks, He broke it and said, "This is My body, which is for you; do this in remembrance of Me." In the same way He took the cup also after supper, saying, "This cup is the new covenant in My blood; do this, as often as you drink it, in remembrance of Me." For as often as you eat this bread and drink the cup, you proclaim the Lord's death until He comes. (1 Corinthians 11:23–26)

When Paul penned these words, the cross was in the past. Jesus had already ascended to heaven, and Paul was writing to the church to let them know how they were to function in both Christ's physical absence as well as His spiritual presence.

One of the statements Paul uses near the beginning lets them know, as well as us, that Communion—the cup and the bread—is "for you." He didn't say it was simply for the purpose of symbolism or for ritual but rather that it is personal. Paul quoted Jesus, saying that Communion is a tangible yet symbolic reflection of the accomplishments of the cross, the benefits of which we will utilize in our daily lives. It is an individual, intimate act of communing with God, even though many people may do it all at the same time.

By personalizing Communion at the onset, we as the participants are ushered into a deeper level of intimacy with the Savior. Sadly, such interaction can be lost in our traditions. Paul reminds his readers of this by including the emphasis that the cross, and also Communion, is for each of us individually as a personal experience with God Himself.

Not only does he remind them (and us) of this, but he uses another term to weave it more so into the context of our lives: "often." This is when Paul quotes Christ as saying, "as often as you drink it" (v. 25). The word "often" used here implies something being done on a regular basis. In other words, Communion ought to be a regular event in each of our lives because the term "often" does not indicate occasional usage. It's not as often as you want to but rather as often as you can.

The Cup of the Covenant

Not only is it important to view Communion through the grid of a personal, ongoing experience, but it is also important to view it through the lens of the covenant. Many of the issues that arise in our lives that we are unable to overcome exist simply because we have failed to realize and apply the covenantal nature of the cross. The act of Communion reminds us of the cross and the new covenant that bestows God's grace.

First, though, we must understand what a covenant is, so we can know what we are supposed to have, develop, and access in our relationship with Jesus Christ over time. For most people, a covenant is simply a formal contractual arrangement. While this is true about the nature of a covenant, a covenant involves much more than that. In the Bible, a covenant is a spiritually binding relationship between God and His people inclusive of certain agreements, conditions, benefits, and effects. It is a divinely created bond.

Whenever God wanted to formalize His relationship with His people, He would establish a covenant. There are a number of these agreements in the Bible, such as the Abrahamic covenant, the Mosaic covenant, the Davidic covenant, and the new covenant. The new covenant is what Paul names in the passage we just looked at referring to Communion: "This cup is the new covenant in My blood"—a reference to Jesus' words during His last supper with the disciples (see Matthew 26:27–28), spoken before His sacrifice on the cross, an event we commemorate during Communion.

These are formal arrangements that are spiritually binding in a legal capacity between God and His people. A good way to grasp the concept of a covenant is the relationship that a man has with a woman when they enter into a marriage union. Prior to that marriage, a legal bond did not exist between them founded on mutually binding agreements and commitments. However, after entering into marriage, the two are now legally bound with set expectations and agreements.

Through the cross, every Christian has entered into a new, unique covenantal bond with God. Recalling the cross through Communion reminds us of the new covenant and God's goodness to His own, and it provides us with the fuel we need for all of life's situations.

A covenant is designed to bring you good. God's new covenant secured through the cross has the same intent. Significantly, Communion serves as a reminder and a renewing of the covenant Christ secured for us on the cross. In Deuteronomy, we read this insight into the beneficial nature of a covenant where it says, "So keep the words of this covenant to do them, that you may prosper in all that you do" (29:9). Yet since the covenant carries with it such great weight and intended blessing, it is not something that was entered into lightly.

Throughout Scripture, a sacrifice of blood was often the requirement for the establishment of a covenant. In one of the earliest covenants, God required Abraham to kill a heifer, goat, and ram, and then He walked between them and uncut birds as a sign of His covenant with Abraham (then Abram), signaling a new relationship with Abraham and his descendants, called the Abrahamic covenant (Genesis 15:5–21). Similarly, the covenantal bond secured through the cross, known as the new covenant, has required the shedding of Christ's blood. When we look at Paul's letter to the church at Corinth in the tenth chapter, we see this where it says, "Is not the cup of blessing which we bless a sharing in the blood of Christ? Is not the bread which we break a sharing in the body of Christ?" (v. 16).

In mentioning the "cup of blessing," Paul is referring to the Communion cup that allows us to share in the life of Christ. Just as a couple in the covenant of marriage experience a deeper level of intimacy in their sexual union, so the cup and the bread are to bring each of us to a new level of intimate sharing in the life of Christ.

Communion allows us to participate more deeply in this relationship with our Savior. In observing Communion there is a more intimate fellowship that is apart from the regular—a superior level of intimacy that God offers to His people. Communion makes the historical event of the cross active in the current life of the believer.

Proclaiming Victory

But not only are we to share in a special level of intimacy with God through Communion, in doing so we benefit from and proclaim the sacrificial power of Jesus' death. As Paul wrote, "For as often as you eat this bread and drink the cup, you proclaim the Lord's death until He comes" (1 Corinthians 11:26). Paul declared that the act of taking Communion is also the act of proclaiming a critical truth. The question that comes out of that, though, is: Proclaim it to whom? And for what reason?

To proclaim something is similar to preaching it or speaking it for others to hear. So what Paul is telling you when you take of the bread and the cup at Communion is that you are at that time preaching your own sermon on the totality of Christ's death. At that moment in the service, you are the preacher. You are the one proclaiming to observers that truth of Christ's great sacrifice—and to Satan and his demons—that your victory has been secured just as Jesus did after He died on the cross (1 Peter 3:19).

We know that the audience you are proclaiming it to includes Satan and his demons because Colossians 2 tells us that on the cross, Christ "disarmed" the rulers and authorities in Satan's realm through His death and resurrection. On the cross, the devil was defeated. Jesus secured the certain victory over the principalities of this world and cleansed you of all penalties for your sin. We read,

> When you were dead in your transgressions and the uncircumcision of your flesh, He made you alive together with Him, having forgiven us all our transgressions, having canceled out the certificate of debt consisting of decrees against us, which was hostile to us; and He has taken it out of the way, having nailed it to the cross. When He had disarmed the rulers and au-

thorities, He made a public display of them, having triumphed over them through Him. (vv. 13–15)

This passage tells us that on the cross, the devil was defeated. He still has more power than you and I do, but the key to understanding spiritual victory in any realm—whether it is in your marriage, career, or elsewhere—is to recognize that power means nothing when you understand authority. On the cross, the devil lost his authority. Jesus "disarmed the rulers and authorities."

So when you take Communion, you are proclaiming to the demonic realm that it no longer has any legitimate right to your life. What the cross means is that the devil was defeated, and what Communion does is remind you of this reality and truth. You need to be reminded of this regularly as does Satan, because the demonic realm does not want to think of themselves as defeated. Nor do they want to relate to you as defeated. Through Communion, God wants you to serve notice and proclaim the true message of the cross to those spiritual forces working against you.

Much of the pain you experience in your life comes from the satanic realm. When you hear someone say, "That ain't nothing but the devil," that's probably true (Ephesians 6:12). Whatever the issue or strife might be is coming from that realm. The satanic realm seeks to invade your realm order to keep you from experiencing all that the cross covenantally provides. So you need to send a message—based on the cup and the bread that represent the victory accomplished for you by Christ on the cross—that hell has lost.

We can understand the current covenantal implications of Communion through another historical context of marriage. Every time a married couple is intimate, they are remembering their wedding day. They are not going back and having a ceremony but they are remembering and renewing the covenant in the current act of sexual intimacy. So what Paul is suggesting to us today is that through Communion, he wants you to remember what happened on the cross—and utilize its power in your daily life.

Be careful not to make into ritual what is supposed to be sacred. Or to turn something profound into something common. Most of us have dining rooms in our house and in those dining rooms are places that hold special china. Your elegant pieces of china aren't dishes for every-day use. Kids can't say, "Make me a ham sandwich and go pull out that china, Mom." They can't do that because the china is special.

Instead, in your kitchen you also have everyday plates. These are the plates that you don't mind as much if they get broken. It has become less significant because its value is less unique.

When Communion is treated with the reverence, intensity, and intimacy that the significance of its covenant entails, the practice of it will uniquely connect us to accomplishments of Christ's covenantal death and resurrection. Even more than that, it provides the opportunity to let the enemy know he no longer holds authority over you.

Two Tables

The apostle Paul takes us even deeper into the all-out spiritual battle that takes place around Communion when he speaks of two tables in the tenth chapter of 1 Corinthians. It says,

> Is not the cup of blessing which we bless a sharing in the blood of Christ? Is not the bread which we break a sharing in the body of Christ? Since there is one bread, we who are many are one body; for we all partake of the one bread. Look at the nation Israel; are not those who eat the sacrifices sharers in the altar?

171

What do I mean then? That a thing sacrificed to idols is any-thing, or that an idol is anything? No, but I say that the things which the Gentiles sacrifice, they sacrifice to demons and not to God; and I do not want you to become sharers in demons. You cannot drink the cup of the Lord and the cup of demons; you cannot partake of the table of the Lord and the table of demons. (vv. 16–21)

Paul makes the point that fellowship with a pagan idol is like having fellowship with demons, which cancels out the benefits that Communion is designed to bring to the believer. Although we do not worship stone idols, we have our own idols in the twenty-first century, for an idol is any unauthorized person, place, or thing that you look to apart from God to get your needs met. So be careful; you may disqualify yourself from the benefits of Communion if you come to the table with another idol in your heart rather than God Almighty.

Let us be careful not to lessen the significance of Communion through failing to take seriously the covenantal commitment that comes through the cross. Remember, the significance of Communion is tied to the significance of the cross whose aim was the defeat of Satan, the for-giveness of sin, the transformation of life, and the flow of blessing. All of that comes wrapped up in the new covenant through what we call grace.

Communion offers you strength where you once knew only weak-ness, through unique, personal fellowship with our Savior as we recall and also benefit from His loving sacrifice. Just as Paul states the conse-quences of taking Communion improperly (weaknesses, sickness, and early death; 1 Corinthians 11:30), there are benefits that come to the believer in these same areas. Communion is God's ordained channel for spiritual well-being.

"Choose Wisely"

I always enjoy a good movie, and the Indiana Jones movies (four in all) are some of my all-time favorites. Harrison Ford really had that character down. The movie I love best in this series is *The Last Crusade*, where Indy and his father search for the holy grail. This was when Indy went in search for the cup of blessing, supposedly the cup Jesus drank from during the Last Supper (and part of King Arthur legend). As he made his way to find this favored cup, multiple enemies sought to stop him and defeat him.

As the film comes to a close, Indy's father lies dying with nothing to save him except the healing power of the cup of blessing itself. Knowing this, Indy speeds toward the location where the cup is well guarded, stepping out in faith and making it through the myriad of death traps. Eventually, Indy arrives at the place where all the cups reside, only to be confronted by the guardian of the grail.

Two profound words come from the guardian's mouth as Indy scours the area, looking for which cup to choose. He says clearly, "Choose wisely." One of the enemies now at the hidden location does not choose wisely, and as a result he disintegrates before their very eyes. Knowing that not only his own life but also his father's rested on his decision, Indiana Jones looks for the cup that Jesus would have used. This is because only the cup of Christ would bring the blessing. (And yes, Indy succeeds and his father recovers.)

Friend, the cross has accomplished a lot for you and me. However, God has given us a choice in our lives. He doesn't force the cup of blessing upon us. He doesn't demand that we drink from His cup and eat from His table. Rather, He offers it along with all of the intensity and authenticity of a covenantal bond with Him. When we drink from it and eat of the bread, we are reminded of the power and grace afforded through Jesus' death on the cross. And as we recognize and proclaim our alignment with His victory on the cross, we will be able to bring healing to our own lips and life and, by His grace and power, to those around us.

12

THE BLESSINGS

A WEALTHY MAN who had lost his wife and later his only son lived several years before he himself died. Over the course of his life, he had accumulated a number of expensive, valuable, and rare commodities, which, following his death, were to be auctioned off in an estate sale. Knowing of the man's taste and choice of exquisite furniture and art, hundreds of people showed up for this auction.

The day began, though, with a piece that most showed no interest in at all. The auctioneer had come forward with a cheaply framed picture of the man's only son, saying, "The first piece we're offering today is this portrait of the man's son." He paused to give everyone a chance to view it, then continued. "Do I have a bid?"

The room fell silent, as no one raised their hands to bid on this framed portrait. They had come for some of the expensive art pieces and artifacts, not for something as simple as that. The auctioneer stood still, not saying a word—something auctioneers will rarely be seen doing—but he could tell on the faces of the attendees that this wasn't something anyone really wanted to buy. So he asked once more, "Do I have a bid? Does anyone want this portrait of the man's son?"

Just then, from the back of the room, an elderly man stepped forward and said, "Sir, I was the servant of the man who died, and if nobody will take the picture of his son, I want to know if I can have it."

The auctioneer said, "One more time. Is there anyone who will bid on the picture of the son?" Yet nobody did. So he then said, "Yes, sir," to the servant, "the picture is yours." The elderly servant slowly walked forward to take hold of the picture of the man's son. Looking lovingly on the boy's image, he then tucked it under his arm and headed toward the back of the room. As he did, though, and to everyone's shock, the auctioneer then picked up his gavel, banged it down, and said, "The auction is now over."

Everybody looked around. Then a couple of would-be bidders asked, "What? You haven't brought out any of the expensive pieces that are supposed to be sold. How can the auction be over?

The auctioneer replied, "The father's will says that the auction was to begin with the picture of his son, and whoever took that got everything else in his estate. He valued his son so highly that he stipulated that whoever took his son's picture would inherit everything.

"Essentially, he who has the son has everything else," the auctioneer summarized. "He who does not have the son, gets nothing."

Sometimes we are like those buyers at the estate auction. We're going around looking for everything else to buy, but God is there, saying, "I have come to give life, and to give it to you more abundantly. But that life can only be found in connection with My Son. If you have My Son, you have eternal life and all that goes with it." It states this so clearly for us in the book of Romans where we read, "He who did not spare His own Son, but delivered Him over for us all, how will He not also with Him freely give us all things?" (8:32).

> THE CROSS PURCHASED FOR US OUR ETERNAL SALVATION BUT ALSO A WHOLE LOT MORE.

All the things that the Lord wants to give to you are entirely connected to His Son, Jesus Christ, and what was accomplished through His death, burial, and resurrection. The cross purchased for us our eternal salvation and freedom from the penalties associated with sin, but it also purchased a whole lot more. These are the things that I like to call the "blessings of the cross," and there are many. These are the "abundant" things that Christ came to give. As Jesus Himself states, "I came that they may have life, and have it abundantly" (John 10:10).

The great thing about the abundance and increase that the Father wants you to have is that it comes, according to the passage in Romans, free of charge: "Will He not also with Him freely give us all things?" In case you didn't catch that, free means absolutely no charge. Yet while it comes with no charge, it also only comes as connected to God's Son and the accomplishment He procured on the cross.

We live in a day of blessing. We live in a so-called Christian culture where sermons galore are spoken on how you can be blessed. Many in Christianity will teach on the blessing unrelated to any connection to Jesus Christ, yet Scripture is explicitly clear that the goodness, favor, and increase in your life and mine comes through one funnel only—the cross of Christ. If all you want are the treasures and the trinkets, but you don't want to be intimately tied to Jesus and all He entails, including the cross, then you are like the men and women standing at the estate sale, disregarding the one and only thing that can bring you everything.

His Blessings Await Us

When the Bible tells us these words, "He who did not spare His own Son," it is giving us insight into the intricate tie that the cross has to our blessings in life. In other words, God did not hold Jesus back from offering Him as a sacrifice—because Christ's sacrifice is the only way by which God can freely give us all things, in light of His character of holiness. God did not stay the nails and the spear as He did Abraham's knife when He spared Isaac. What God did for Isaac, He didn't even do for His own blood, love, and essence.

When you learn to view life's blessings through that harsh but necessary sacrifice, it brings about a level of gratitude that is more in line with what we have truly received. It makes a connection for us that we don't always keep at the forefront of our minds. And it highlights one of the purposes of the cross in such a way so it becomes virtually impossible to view God's favor apart from His mercy and grace. The cross of Christ is the entryway to all the things God has determined for your life.

As I've mentioned before, our God is not bound in time. He knows the end from the beginning. He has already established and prepared your blessings in life. We see in Ephesians: "Blessed be the God and Father of our Lord Jesus Christ, who has blessed us with every spiritual blessing in the heavenly places in Christ" (1:3). The word used for "blessed" in that verse is past tense. That is a critical distinction to recognize; otherwise you may view life and God's goodness as something you have to personally earn or achieve. However, God's blessings have already been decided for you. They have already been placed in a room with your name on it in the "heavenly places." The only key needed to access those blessings is faith in the finished work of Christ—faith in all that Christ has accomplished for you and all that God desires to do on your behalf.

Too many believers may one day get to heaven and be taken, figuratively, to this room only to discover that we did not fully access all the goodness God had designed for us to receive and fulfill. This is because too many of us have limited or no real authentic connection to the Christ of the cross. Without Christ, the "all things" remain removed and distant. With Christ, there is an ever-increasing flow of God's power, wisdom, delight, and blessings both to you and through you.

I can understand in our opening story of the estate sale how the portrait of the son didn't look like much in the eyes of most. It didn't seem to offer much. The hundreds of people in attendance did not jump in to bid on that item, for how could they have known? However, with Christ and the cross, God has made it very clear what comes to us through His Son. "He who has the Son has the life" (1 John 5:11–12), the apostle wrote. The Scriptures make it clear that the cross is not one of many things we are to cherish most; it is the thing. It is everything. Without it, neither grace nor mercy has a pathway to our lives.

That's why Paul wrote so clearly, "For I determined to know nothing among you except Jesus Christ, and Him crucified" (1 Corinthians 2:2). In stating this, Paul reminds us of the central nature of the cross. He reminds us that you don't get to the "all things" in life by going after all things. You get to the all things through the one thing, the cross where Jesus was crucified.

Christ's Character in Us

One of the more popularly quoted passages in Scripture is Romans 8:28, "And we know that God causes all things to work together for good to those who love God, to those who are called according to His purpose." Yet, what is often missed is the truth that shows up in the very next verse, "For those whom He foreknew, He also predestined to become conformed to the image of His Son, so that He would be the firstborn among many brethren." Here is God's goal stated for us: God's goal is to clone the character of Jesus Christ in us—in you. His desire is for you to "become conformed to the image of His Son." That means you and I are to essentially mirror Christ. We are to increasingly look like Him in our attitudes, character, and conduct.

God wants some look-alikes. He loves Jesus so much that He wants His own to resemble Him. And when they do, He causes "all things to work together for good." All things. There is that phrase once again.

God's purpose for you is that everything that happens in your life is to make you look like Jesus Christ. Keep in mind that includes the good, the bad, and the ugly. You are not just to look at what happened to you on face value. You are to look at the situations, circumstances, and relationships in your life with this question in mind: God, how do you want to use this (good, bad, or ugly) to make me more conformed to the character of Christ?

It's easy to want to get rid of the negative realities in our lives, or to remove the burdens from our backs and throw away the trials. But the thought that should accompany every experience is if God is amalgamating the "all things" for good, then how does He want to use this particular situation in that equation? Remember, He wants to conform you to Christ so that you can pass through the gate of the cross and access the "all things" God has determined to bless you with.

Yes, developing His character in us may mean pain at times. When a baby is born with a crooked leg, months later a doctor will often place that growing child into leg braces. The doctor wants to work with the growth process to straighten the leg. For the child, it's often hard to sleep in those braces, and it may be uncomfortable to walk in them, but the goal of the braces is to conform the legs toward the path of its proper developmental position.

Those braces, though annoying, cumbersome, and sometimes even painful, have a greater purpose in mind—to strengthen the legs to bring the child greater benefit, enjoyment, and freedom than he would have by being left to his own.

When God works all things together for our good, that doesn't mean that the "all things" are necessarily favorable in and of themselves.

But the goal of the all things is to produce an environment wherein you can fully benefit, enjoy, and experience the full freedom of your destiny.

One way you will truly know that you are fully living out the blessings of the cross is when the "all things" that come your way, including the painful, no longer dictate your life. Just a few verses after Romans 8:28, Paul takes us to another set of "all things," but this time these things are not good, as perceived by mankind. He writes, "Just as it is written,

> YOU HAVE ACCESSED THE BLESSINGS OF THE CROSS WHEN YOU ARE NOW CONQUERING THINGS THAT USED TO CONQUER YOU.

'For Your sake we are being put to death all day long; We were considered as sheep to be slaughtered.' But in all these things we overwhelmingly conquer through Him who loved us" (vv. 36–37).

This is how you know you have accessed the blessings of the cross, when you are now conquering things that used to conquer you. Stuff that used to be in charge of your emotions, time, and thoughts you are now in charge of. That which used to control you, you are now controlling.

That is the definition of a true blessing. A blessing doesn't always come wrapped in a shiny box or with a fast engine. The greatest blessings in life include the ability to enjoy peace and stability in spite of circumstances. They include strength of character and strength of mind. These are the blessings that will bring you the greatest joy and victory, for when you experience these blessings, you will discover the delight of life. You will know what true abundance really is.

Anyone who has ever watched pro wrestling for any length of time realizes that these battles are pre-scripted. Prior to any wrestler stepping into the ring, both the conqueror and the loser have been determined. However, the process of arriving at that victory still has its ups and downs, its twists and turns. Between the opening bell and the conclusion, there will be real bumps, bruises, and some battering along the way. But all of these things are working together toward the good of a predetermined end.

God has already predetermined your life and both the future and hope that He has for you (Jeremiah 29:11). Yet how you fare in the ring on your way to victory is largely tied to whether you are living out your life's purpose of being conformed to Jesus Christ and His cross.

The Big Gift

Jim and Julie had been dating steadily for some time when he decided to take her out to a fancy restaurant. Julie got all excited when he invited her and announced he loved her. Then he added, "I have something extra special for you that night."

After they arrived at the nice restaurant that Saturday, he went back to his car to grab the gift. He returned with a very large box, too large to set it on the table. He set it on the floor beside them. Knowing that most "special" gifts come in small packages, Julie was confused, but she trusted what he had told her and tried to enjoy the meal.

As their nice dinner came to a close, he presented the gift. Julie daintily took off the ribbon, wondering what was inside. She lifted the lid, expecting just what he had said—something extra special. That's when she saw it. It was a pillow.

"You got me a pillow?" she asked, trying not to let her disappointment show.

"Well, not really," he said.

Her eyes stared back, telling him to please continue.

"That's my pillow," he continued. More silence met his words. But that was when he lovingly took the pillow from her hands, placed it on the floor beside her, knelt down on it, and asked her to marry him.

"I want to know," he said as she fought back tears, "if you will allow me the privilege of spending the rest of my life with you."

That pillow didn't look like much when she first opened it. To her, it had no meaning. But when the pillow was used for a special purpose, nothing turned into everything.

Sometimes the cross may not look like much to us. In many of our minds it's just some wood from another culture in an ancient day. But when you understand that there is a whole lot more to this thing than what it looks like, and when you use it properly connected with who was on it, the cross becomes everything. Through the power of the cross, God will freely give you all things. "Nothing much" quickly turns into everything when you use it right.

Paid in Full

Mr. Lowe was excited as he boarded the luxury ship for his very first cruise. He had saved for this four-day cruise, yet the ticket was so costly he had no extra money to spend on food after buying his ticket. When he saw everyone else eating the next day, he felt bad because he was so hungry. Having packed some sardines and crackers for his four-day excursion, he returned to his cabin and ate alone, while everyone else enjoyed the first of many lavish meals.

On the last day of the trip, he made his way to the kitchen, his stomach snarling in complaint. Mr. Lowe asked one of the cooks if he could just get a sandwich. That's when the cook looked at him in disbelief and replied, "You didn't know that when you bought your ticket that the price of the food was included in the fare?"

Everything this man needed was there for him to enjoy, he just didn't know he could access it.

On the cross, God has paid the price for the "all things" in your life. And these things He has promised to freely give to you through Jesus Christ. You don't have to go buy it, earn it, or be perfect to get it. It comes through faith in the shed blood of Jesus through what God has termed as grace.

Whenever you are tempted to question the love of God, He invites you instead to look at the cross. He says, in essence, "If I didn't spare My own Son—if I loved you enough to do that, then there ought never to be a question again about how much I love you. Trust Me. I'm working these things out toward good."

How much does God love you? He loves you to death—even death on a cross. When you and I incorporate this truth of the cross into every aspect of our lives, we will be able to recognize the presence of God's blessings in our lives. Otherwise, we will forever be mixing doubt with faith, tainting the faith and thus removing its power to access God's grace. For "without faith it is impossible to please" God (Hebrews 11:6).

The Way of the Cross

I wish that I could tell you that the road to experiencing all things is going to be seamless, without problems. I wish that I could write that in good conscience, but I can't. The Bible's position on that is my position: God never promises us a yellow brick road free of trial. It's true that many preaching prosperity and blessing try to paint that picture of a road to favor, void of conflict or pain. But since that is not what God says, that is not what I will say.

You may want a resurrection Sunday in your life, as we all do. But bear in mind that there is no resurrection Sunday without a Friday . . . and the cross. Jesus was not highly exalted by God until after Calvary. He had to go through great pain to be able to help us through our own.

The blessing of a resurrection can only come through connection to the cross. You can't rise from the dead if you haven't died. Neither can God resurrect things in your life whether it be a career, relationship, your heart, finances, health—anything—without your public connection with the cross.

No matter how ugly, how unpolitically correct, and how offensive it may seem to some, the pain of the cross is the only way to its power and joy in the Christian life.

The Scars of Love

One day a woman got caught in a vicious hailstorm. The large hailstones fell fast and furious, so hard on her that she was not able to run anymore in order to make it indoors. A man inside a nearby store saw her struggling and ran outside. He draped his body over her, absorbing the stones' force as he led her to the store. The hail that would have pummeled her brutally struck him instead.

By the time he was able to safely get her inside, huge welts covered his upper body. One arm was cut and bleeding, and his left cheek was also bleeding from the pounding he took. The woman thanked him and wanted to do something special for this stranger who cared enough to protect her, so she invited him to dinner the next week for a home-cooked meal. One thing led to another, and they eventually fell in love and got married.

One day a friend asked her about the scars on her husband's face and arms, and she told her, "Every morning I wake up, I look over at him and see the scars. I run my fingers up and down the scars because I know that he got those scars protecting me. Those scars are beautiful to me because I know that if he is willing to do that, he's got me covered for anything else that may come at me in the future."

When you and I get to heaven, we will be standing before God in a glorified, perfected form. You and I will be flawless because there are no flaws in heaven, except for one. There will still be one who has scars, and that is Jesus Christ. We will see the scars on His hands from the nailing to the cross, and the scar from the spear in His side. And there will be other marks. We know this because after He rose from the dead and appeared to Thomas in His glorified body, He told Thomas to touch where the spear had gone into His side (John 20:27).

In glory, our God Jesus Christ will have scars—a reminder throughout all of eternity how much He loves you and me. But even now He doesn't want us to lose sight of these scars, because those scars are proof positive that we can go through this life with abundance, overwhelmingly conquering and not simply getting by. The blessings of the cross are found in the scars of the One who loved us enough to give Himself up in order to protect you and me.

THE FINAL VICTORY

THE MYTHICAL STORY is told of two men standing in a marketplace many years ago when the first saw a hideously looking creature come before him. The man looked at his friend and asked, "Who is that?"

His friend replied quickly and somberly, "That's Mr. Death."

As the grotesque being walked even closer to the first man, the man felt himself tremble inside. Unsure what to do or where to go, he said to his friend, "He's coming to me—what do I do?"

"If it were me," his friend replied, "I'd hop a horse and get to the next city in order to escape his grasp."

Which is exactly what the man did, riding off across the countryside filled with both fear and dread. That evening, as he rode into the next town, the man breathed a sigh of relief that he had made it safely away and had successfully beaten Mr. Death—only to discover after catching his breath that this ugly being was standing right in front of him, several paces off.

Dejected and discouraged, the man stood there speechless. As Mr. Death approached him, he said, "I've come to get you." The man replied, "But I saw you in my hometown earlier this morning and came here because I thought I was escaping you!"

That's when Mr. Death responded, "You know what? I am a little curious myself because I saw you in your hometown earlier today as well, but my appointment with you was in this town tonight."

No matter how hard you run, no matter how many miles you jog, or how many weights you lift—or how many glasses of organic fresh-pressed juices you drink—you will never escape Mr. Death. Mr. Death has the ability to locate you wherever you are, and he won't be late. The Bible makes it inextricably clear that "it is appointed for men to die once and after this comes judgment" (Hebrews 9:27). You may be late for a lot of things in your life, but you will be on time for that one. In this world, there is no escaping death.

Of all of the problems that you and I face, and they are many, death by far is the greatest one. Nothing produces more fear, anxiety, or uncertainty than Mr. Death. Mr. Death has a way of messing up good days. No matter how sophisticated we become in our medical care and facilities and no matter how advanced we get in our treatments and medications, we can never fully conquer the grim reaper's effect.

So real and so traumatic is this reality that few of us ever even refer to it as death. Rather, we call it passing away, or laid to rest. And instead of saying that we buried someone in the cemetery, we say we put them in the family plot. It sounds less harsh and less final that way. Yet no matter what the phraseology we choose to use, Mr. Death is just that, death, and he stands by hovering, waiting for his next life to take.

How People Deal with Death

One way humanity has tried to deal with the finality of death is to believe in reincarnation. This is the idea that somehow some mysterious force will bring me back to a second earthly life in some form or another. Perhaps I'll return better than before, perhaps I'll return worse—all based on the lifestyle I live during my first time on earth.

Other people have come up with the belief system that includes purgatory, which involves an area midway between eternal hell and eternal heaven that will allow me another opportunity to escape judgment. And still others just pretend to ignore Mr. Death altogether and simply say that when you are gone, it's over. When you are dead, that's it. They say that life after death doesn't happen at all.

These fears and associations that we have with death are not unfounded in any way. God tells us through His Word that life is like a vapor. We are all "just a vapor that appears for a little while and then vanishes away" (James 4:14). This is similar to fireworks on the Fourth of July that shine brightly for a season, only to dissipate and disappear just as quickly.

The psalmist concluded, "My days have been consumed in smoke" (102:3). And Job said that death is "the king of terrors" (Job 18:14). Death thrives on unpredictability. It could be a car accident, a heart attack, a stroke—even a stray bullet or plane crash. Death doesn't take notice of odds so none of us know when he will appear in our lives.

What does this have to do with the cross, you wonder?

Everything. The cross was necessary for there to be a resurrection. The cross is the great prelude to seeing the Death Conqueror.

Paul writes, "Now if Christ is preached, that He has been raised from the dead, how do some among you say that there is no resurrection of the dead? But if there is no resurrection of the dead, not even Christ has been raised; and if Christ has not been raised, then our preaching is vain, your faith also is vain" (1 Corinthians 15:12–14). Can you see the connection? Paul says that if Christ Himself is risen from the dead, then why are you spending an inordinate amount of time discussing what happens to dead people. If there is no resurrection, then it follows that Jesus Christ is also dead. And if Christ has not been raised, then you ought to close the book, I ought to stop writing, stop preaching, and all of us ought to stop believing. After all, what good is it to believe in someone who is still dead?

Moreover, we become false witnesses of God to say that Christ is raised from the dead if, in fact, the dead are not raised at all. For if the dead are not raised, not even Jesus has been raised. And if Jesus has not been raised, then your faith, and my faith, is a waste of time because you, and I, are still in our sins. Worse off, Paul adds, "Then those also who have fallen asleep in Christ have perished. If we have hoped in Christ in this life only, we are of all men most to be pitied" (vv. 18–19).

> **IT IS IN THE CROSS OF JESUS CHRIST, COUPLED WITH HIS RESURRECTING POWER, THAT WE FIND ETERNAL SALVATION.**

In other words, Paul says that if all Jesus can do is help you in this life, but not the next, then you ought to go find something more. Because everyone needs help beyond this life, not just in it. That is why Paul gave his days, time, efforts, and energies in preaching the cross of Christ. It is in the cross of Jesus Christ, coupled with His resurrecting power, that we find our eternal salvation. Paul goes on to declare this greatest of victories that the cross secured for each of us:

> But now Christ has been raised from the dead, the first fruits of those who are asleep. For since by a man came death, by a man also came the resurrection of the dead. For as in Adam all die, so also in Christ all will be made alive. But each in his own order: Christ the first fruits, after that those who are Christ's at His coming. (vv. 20–23)

In these verses Paul makes the connection of the cross to the victory in the resurrection that is ours as well. Because of what Jesus did both in dying and being raised, Mr. Death no longer has authority over you or me. Friend, I don't know of any better news that I could give to you than this: The victory of the resurrection of Jesus Christ two thousand years ago made the thing you fear the most become the thing that you don't have to fear at all. The good news of the resurrection is that death itself has been overcome.

The Bible tells us in Hebrews 2:15 that Jesus came in order that He "might free those who through fear of death were subject to slavery all their lives." Slavery is not a good thing, on any level. And if death has you frightened in any way, you have become a slave to it. In fact, if you are too scared to fly, even though everything mechanically checks out and the people controlling the instruments are qualified, then you are a slave to death. Whatever unnerves you ultimately rules you.

Yet Paul reminds us that the combination of the cross and the resurrection has conquered death. He tells us this very poetically when he speaks about the time when the perishable puts on the imperishable, and the mortal clothes itself with immortality. At that time, Paul writes, we will each say, "'Death is swallowed up in victory. O death, where is your victory? O death, where is your sting?' The sting of death is sin, and the power of sin is the law; but thanks be to God, who gives us the victory through our Lord Jesus Christ" (1 Corinthians 15:54–56).

Sin, Law, and Death

See, death exists because sin exists. If there were no sin, there would be no death. God told Adam that in the day he ate of the forbidden fruit, he would die (Genesis 3:3). And through Adam, death entered humanity. So the only reason that death even exists is because of sin.

But Paul instructs in the passage we just looked at that "the power of sin is [in] the law." The only reason sin exists is because there is a righteous standard by which to measure it—the law. The one way that you and I even know about sin and what sin is comes as a result of someone telling us about the law. It comes as a result of reading God's Word about His standard. It's a result of knowing and understanding God's law.

For example, the only reason we know that we can be pulled over for a speeding ticket is because there is a sign that gives us a speeding limit. If there is no speeding limit, then there is no speeding ticket. You can only be condemned for breaking the law because there is a law to break. If there is no law, then there is no sin. If there is no sin, then there is no judgment. As we saw in an earlier chapter, the law doesn't exist to make you righteous. It exists to reveal your sin. God didn't give the Ten Commandments so that you can keep them. He gave the Ten Commandments to reveal to each of us how often we break them. The same is true for the law, His standard in our lives. He gave us this standard through His Word and the righteous life of Jesus Christ to show us that we regularly break them in both thought and deed, resulting in sin.

We have all sinned and fallen short of the glory, perfection, and holiness of God (Romans 3:23). And because of that we face what God calls the "wages" of sin, which is death (6:23). So if sin leads to death and we all sin, then if we want to get rid of death, we have to solve the problem of sin. This means the only way to solve the problem of sin is to satisfy the demands of the law.

Because of sin, the only way to satisfy God's divine law so that we would no longer be under the condemnation of death was through a sinless sacrifice. Enter Jesus Christ. And enter the cross and the resurrection that follows. This causes Paul to declare, "Thanks be to God, who gives us the victory through our Lord Jesus Christ" (1 Corinthians 15:57).

CONCLUSION: THE FINAL VICTORY

The victory of the resurrection means that death has been whipped to such a finality that every man, woman, boy, or girl who has a personal relationship with Jesus Christ will never suffer a final death. There is resurrection and being with Jesus. I'm not sure that there is any better news than that on any level. Jesus Christ addressed the law on the cross. In His resurrection He overcame the consequences of breaking that law.

The Perfect Savior, the Perfect Payment

Yet not all of this took place on the cross. Jesus Christ spent thirty-three perfect and sinless years on earth first, because whomever was going to satisfy God had to do so perfectly. That's why Jesus said at His baptism that He had come to fulfill all righteousness (Matthew 3:15). In essence, He came to keep all the law. That's why when you read the Gospels, He is meticulously keeping the law, being perfect in every single detail. By doing so, He qualified Himself to become the Savior of others since He did not have to save Himself. On the cross, Jesus Christ as God's Son—having kept the entirety of the law—bore our sin and conquered death.

When you go to a restaurant and order a meal, the waiter will bring you a bill at the end of your meal. Whether you pay by plastic or cash, once you pay, the waiter will then bring you a receipt acknowledging that not only was payment made but that payment was also accepted. Both of these are important because if your card is not validated when you are paying or your twenty-dollar bill is deemed counterfeit, then your payment will be denied and you will still owe for the meal. In that case, you will need to come up with another payment method.

Jesus' death on the cross not only offered the payment for the sin of all humanity (past, present, and future) but when He cried out, "It is finished," on the cross—the literal translation of those words refers to a debt being paid. It means "paid in full." Christ's payment was accepted. Through this, we know the payment was made. Yet how do we know that His payment was accepted? The resurrection of Jesus Christ is the receipt for the payment on Friday for the debt of the sins of mankind. Jesus Christ is a living record of payment made and accepted.

Removing Death's Sting

Because of Christ's unequivocal payment, we have only one thing to say to Mr. Death: "Where is your sting?" Because as a believer in Jesus Christ, when it is your time to leave this earth, you won't even have a moment of transition. In a twinkling of an eye, you will be in the midst of the perfect Savior's presence. You will be fully revived in your eternal state of being. Essentially, you don't even get to die but rather you move on into the perfection of God Himself.

When you truly come to understand and realize this, death loses its intimidation. When you know that your loved ones who have also trusted in Christ are not gone from you forever, but you will see them again, it takes the edge off of the absence. Sure, you miss them. But eternity is an awfully long time to get caught back up.

A father was driving his son one day when a bee flew in through the open window. The dad knew that his son was severely allergic to bees and out of the corner of his eye saw his boy start to panic. The dad reached out and grabbed the bee, squeezing it in his own hand, and then releasing it. The bee began to dart and buzz around the boy again and the son called out to his dad to help.

"Son, don't worry," his father said. "The bee is making a lot of noise, but it doesn't have any sting left in it." The father opened his hand and showed just where the bee had stung him.

Death still makes a lot of noise in our lives today and in the world around us. But the greatest victory the cross gained for you and for me is that death no longer holds its sting. The resurrection of Jesus Christ means that at the very worst all you can be hit by now when death comes lurking is a shadow, not death itself.

Paul tells us that to be absent from the body is to be present with the Lord (2 Corinthians 5:8). Think about that. When you get that truth deep down in your soul, you realize that as a believer in Jesus Christ and His cross, you don't even get to experience death long enough to know that you died. Less than the time it takes you to blink your eye, you are taken from earth to heaven—suddenly.

When you die it is the beginning and not the end. It is a wedding, and not a funeral. Death is your introduction to new life. And because of the cross, you can face it with courage.

The Victory Is Ours

So what should that truth do for you while you live? Paul gives us that answer as well when he wraps up his treatise on this life-and-death subject. He says, "Therefore, my beloved brethren, be steadfast, immovable, always abounding in the work of the Lord, knowing that your toil is not in vain in the Lord" (1 Corinthians 15:58). This is the resultant effect of Christ's victory over death in our lives. No longer bound by "what-ifs" or fear, we are to be bold, consistent, and driven in our work for the Lord. We have confidence to do this just as an employee has confidence that his or her work will be rewarded with a paycheck at the end of the week or month.

Far too many Christians still live with a question mark when it comes to death. Or they simply deny it altogether in their thoughts. Doing so makes work for the Lord seem cumbersome in many ways. After all, what good does it bring and what return on investment will be seen? But when the reality of eternal life and victory over death is a concrete image in your heart, soul, and mind, working for the Lord makes all the sense in the world. You will see Him face-to-face one day. At that time you will be glad for everything you did in His name. You will get your reward for your dedication and service and love. You will eternally live out what you have put into eternity during time. All of that is true because of the cross and the resurrection. And when you live your life from that vantage point, you will make decisions that reflect His heart, His goals, His viewpoint, and His kingdom agenda on earth.

Friend, live in light of the victory that is yours in Jesus Christ. He gave His all that you might, by His grace and mercy, experience the full manifestation of your own.

EPILOGUE

UNITY AT THE FOOT OF THE CROSS

ATHLETES ON ONE team can work together despite differences in class, race, and belief systems. Alcoholics can get drunk in unity, no matter who is around. Even drug addicts are seen "doing drugs" together across racial lines.

Yet the body of Christ still divides over all those differences, and more. What is at the root of the inability of Christians to unify across color, class, culture, and denomination? I believe it is our failure to truly understand what was achieved for us on the cross.

We do not truly comprehend amazing grace, even though we sing about it. The diminishment of Calvary and all it gained keeps us divided, and as a result it keeps us ineffective for advancing God's kingdom on earth.

As we seek to use the power of the cross in our daily lives, here is a final application: May the truths found through reconciliation with God lead to unity among our churches.

Just prior to His arrest and crucifixion, Jesus prayed for His followers, present and future. His prayer, recorded in John 17, reveals Christ's desire for us, "that they may all be one; even as You, Father, are in Me

197

and I in You, that they also may be in Us, so that the world may believe that You sent Me" (v. 21). Christ's prayer was that when He left this earth, God would bring about unity in history through the church. Christ knew that if those outside the church saw us—we who are so different in so many ways—being one in unity, then they would have to believe that God indeed sent Jesus Christ, His Son. The purpose of the unity achieved for us through the cross is so that the world may know that Jesus is real.

Jesus' high priestly prayer makes it contingent on the church to have a functional unity in order to visually demonstrate His validity before the world. If the church does not show such unity, the opposite outcome is true as well: The lack of harmony among us discredits Jesus Christ and the cross.

So vital was this prayer that God made its content—unity in love—a criterion for the full experience of our relationship with Him. We see this in the apostle John's first letter: "If someone says, 'I love God,' and hates his brother, he is a liar; for the one who does not love his brother whom he has seen, cannot love God whom he has not seen. And this commandment we have from Him, that the one who loves God should love his brother also" (1 John 4:20–21). In other words, we can't have one without the other. Our fellowship and intimacy with God hinges on our relationship with each other. It is more than Christ's prayer before giving His all on the cross, it is a commandment. Unity—oneness—in the body of Christ is a commandment.

Many people are calling for a revival in our nation, myself included. The problems that plague us loom larger than ever before. We stand on the precipice of severe consequences for national choices that have collectively impacted us all. Yet one thing remains missing in the body of Christ that must appear before revival can occur, and that is unity. God is not going to bless a disunified, schizophrenic church. He won't bless a racist church, a classist church, or even a legalistic church. At the foot of the cross, we all stand on even ground—saved by faith alone in Christ alone. That is the oneness for which Jesus prayed, and for which Jesus died.

Nowhere else is this truth made so clear as in my favorite book of the Bible, Ephesians. In Ephesians, we are given the theology of unity. We are taught about the greatest power of the cross, after salvation, and we are called to our highest purpose, making Christ and His death and resurrection known to *others through our love for one another*. We read,

> But now in Christ Jesus you who formerly were far off have been brought near by the blood of Christ. For He Himself is our peace, who made both groups into one and broke down the barrier of the dividing wall, by abolishing in His flesh the enmity, which is the Law of commandments contained in ordinances, so that in Himself He might make the two into one new man, thus establishing peace, and might reconcile them both in one body to God through the cross, by it having put to death the enmity. (2:13–16)

On the cross, Jesus broke down our dividing walls. He established our peace. He bought our oneness with His own blood. That is why we have been called to "preserve" the peace rather than to create it. Our oneness has already been created in Christ Jesus through the cross, so it is to the cross we must turn if we are going to experience it. Paul describes this oneness in Ephesians 4: "With all humility and gentleness, with patience, showing tolerance for one another in love, being diligent to preserve the unity of the Spirit in the bond of peace" (vv. 2–3).

We have not been asked to find unity or figure out how to hold reconciliation seminars. What we have been asked to do is to come

THE POWER OF THE CROSS

humbly, gently, and patiently to the foot of the cross to preserve the unity that Christ *has already bought* for us with His death. According to the Scripture, Jesus has already established our peace, removed our hostilities, and broken down our walls. There is no longer "Jew nor Greek, . . . male nor female" (Galatians 3:28). Not when we are all at the foot of the cross.

If we will simply live out in humility the unity Christ has secured for us, we can not only transform our families, churches, and communities but we can collectively transform our entire nation and the world. The cross is the power for our victory. But we can only access that joint power through unity.

I'm sure you know that oil and water don't mix. Actually, they don't normally mix. There is an exception. The exception occurs when you add an emulsifier to oil and water, such as an egg. What the egg does is bind with the oil and bind with the water and thus bind them both together. In our culture today, we are comprised of so many different ethnicities, backgrounds, stations in life, preferences, and denominations that we wind up each pursuing our own platforms, segmented from each other while failing to make a unified impact for God. What Christ did at the cross was become our emulsifier. In Him, although our differences remain, we find what binds us together for a common good.

Unity is never uniformity. Unity is oneness of purpose. The purpose of the unity achieved at the cross was so that the world may know that Jesus is the Christ, the Son of God. That is our purpose, yet that is what we fail to broadcast and proclaim when we remain divided across so many plains.

The cross accomplished so much for us, as we have seen throughout this book. The cross provides power, blessing, grace, and so much more. But there is only one thing Jesus said would make Him known to all the nations and that is the unified peace He achieved for us on the cross.

Our division is not just a disappointment to God; it is disobedience. If we don't get anything else right in the body of Christ, we must learn how to get this right. Because without it, Christ's death, burial, and resurrection goes unnoticed and unknown to so many who need Him as their Lord and Savior.

Jesus paid the ultimate price for our benefit and our gain when He gave His life on the cross. Don't we owe Him everything? Shouldn't we seek to make Him known? It is my prayer that we as a body of believers will learn not only to embrace our peace but also how to truly function as one.

THE URBAN ALTERNATIVE

DR. TONY EVANS and The Urban Alternative (TUA) **equips, empowers,** and **unites** Christians to **impact** *individuals, families, churches,* and *communities* to restore hope and transform lives.

We believe the core cause of the problems we face in our personal lives, homes, churches, and societies is a spiritual one; therefore, the only way to address them is spiritually. We've tried a political, a social, an economic, and even a religious agenda. It's time for a Kingdom Agenda—God's visible and comprehensive rule over every area of life because when we function as we were designed, there is a divine power that changes everything. It renews and restores as the life of Christ is made manifest within our own. As we align ourselves under Him, there is an alignment that happens from deep within—where He brings about full restoration. It is an atmosphere that revives and makes whole.

As it impacts us, it impacts others—transforming every sphere of life in which we live. When each biblical sphere of life functions in accordance with God's Word, the outcomes are evangelism, discipleship, and community impact. As we learn how to govern ourselves under God, we then transform the institutions of family, church, and society from a biblically based kingdom perspective, where through Him, we are touching heaven and changing earth.

To achieve our goal we use a variety of strategies, methods, and resources for reaching and equipping as many people as possible.

Broadcast Media

Hundreds of thousands of individuals experience *The Alternative with Dr. Tony Evans* through the daily radio broadcast playing on nearly one thousand radio outlets in more than one hundred countries. The broadcast can also be seen on several television networks, and is viewable online at TonyEvans.org.

Leadership Training

The Kingdom Agenda Pastors (KAP) provides a *viable network* for *like-minded pastors* who embrace the Kingdom Agenda philosophy. Pastors have the opportunity to go deeper with Dr. Tony Evans as they are given greater biblical knowledge, practical applications, and resources to impact individuals, families, churches, and communities. KAP welcomes *senior and associate pastors* of all churches.

The Kingdom Agenda Pastors' Summit progressively develops church leaders to meet the demands of the twenty-first century while maintaining the gospel message and the strategic position of the church. The Summit introduces *intensive seminars, workshops,* and *resources,* addressing issues affecting the community, family, leadership, organizational health, and more.

Pastors' Wives Ministry, founded by Dr. Lois Evans, provides *counsel, encouragement,* and *spiritual resources* for pastors' wives as they serve with their husbands in the ministry. A primary focus of the ministry is the KAP Summit that offers senior pastors' wives a safe place to *reflect, renew,* and *relax* along with training in personal development, spiritual growth, and care for their emotional and physical well-being.

Community Impact

National Church Adopt-A-School Initiative (NCAASI) prepares churches across the country to impact communities by using *public schools as the primary vehicle for effecting positive social change* in urban youth and families. Leaders of churches, school districts, faith-based organizations, and other nonprofit organizations are equipped with the knowledge and tools to *forge partnerships* and build *strong social service delivery systems.* This training is based on the comprehensive church-based community impact strategy conducted by Oak Cliff Bible Fellowship. It addresses such areas as economic development, education, housing, health revitalization, family renewal, and racial reconciliation. We also assist churches in tailoring the model to meet the specific needs of their communities while simultaneously addressing the spiritual and moral frame of reference.

Resource Development

We are fostering lifelong learning partnerships with the people we serve by providing a variety of published materials. We offer booklets, Bible studies, books, CDs, and DVDs to strengthen people in their walk with God and ministry to others.

* * *

For more information, a catalog of Dr. Tony Evans'
ministry resources,
and a complimentary copy of Dr. Evans' devotional newsletter,
call (800) 800-3222
or write TUA at P.O. Box 4000, Dallas TX 75208,
or log on to
*www.*TonyEvans.org

EVANS
THE URBAN ALTERNATIVE

At The Urban Alternative, the national ministry of Dr. Tony Evans, we seek to restore hope and transform lives to reflect the values of the kingdom of God. Along with our community outreach initiative, leadership training and family and personal growth emphasis, Dr. Evans continues to minister to people from the pulpit to the heart as the relevant expositor with the powerful voice. Lives are touched both locally and abroad through our daily radio broadcast, weekly television ministry and internet access points.

PRESENTING AN
ALTERNATIVE TO:

COMMUNITY OUTREACH

Equipping leaders to engage public schools and communities with mentoring, family support services and a commitment to a brighter tomorrow.

LEADERSHIP TRAINING

Offering an exclusive opportunity for pastors and their wives to receive discipleship from Drs. Tony and Lois Evans and the TUA staff, along with networking opportunities, resources and encouragement.

FAMILY AND PERSONAL GROWTH

Strengthening homes and deepening spiritual lives through helpful resources that encourage hope and health for the glory of God.

TONYEVANS.ORG

THE KINGDOM AGENDA

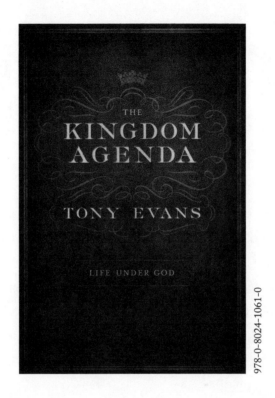

978-0-8024-1061-0

God's kingdom isn't just about theology and church. It isn't just a quaint religious idea or an obscure theological concept. It is about a whole new way of seeing the world and your place in it. As God's people, we are not limited by the choices this world offers us. God has an alternative plan for us— His kingdom with an all-encompassing agenda.

The Kingdom Agenda offers a fresh and powerful vision that will help you think differently about your life, your relationships, and your walk with God. When you start with a kingdom agenda, living in relationship with the true King and embracing your place in His Kingdom, nothing will ever be the same.

MOODY
Publishers™

From the Word to Life

urbanpraise

Urban Praise, a commercial-free Moody Radio Internet station, offers a soulful blend of rich gospel and urban music. Energize your faith with artists like Kirk Franklin, Israel Houghton, Shirley Caesar, CeCe Winans, Walter Hawkins, and Lecrae, along with bite-size teaching segments from Tony Evans, Crawford Loritts, Melvin Banks, Beth Moore, and others.

www.urbanpraiseradio.org

MOODY
Radio™

From the Word to Life